'*A town of a by-gone era, a town steeped in history, now but a memory for those that walked it.*'

Kevin M. Hall

ISBN: 9798448556739

Ilion, My Childhood, My Memories

Front Cover Design explanation:

Often times a book reader will glance at a book cover and get an idea of what the book content might be about. Sometimes the reader will skip the front cover and go right to the back cover to read a brief paragraph or two regarding the books content.

As the author I put a number of messages into the design of this front cover. First note that the cover is split between Black and White and Color pictures. This was done purposely to show the historical – black and white photos, versus the existing – color photos; the historical now being but a memory of the author and it is those memories that are the main content of this book.

The color picture of the Ilion Library – largest building at top of the book represents the location of the historical documents about the town of Ilion, and the town historian being very knowledgeable of town events and historical timelines. Therefore, the library represents the largest hub for village historical research and was a great resource in the researching needed to complete this book.

The color pictures of the other buildings are meant as a question by the author for the reader. The fact is that these buildings were within the identified acreage that was the subject of Urban Renewal (UR) and its resultant razing of 113 buildings, however:

- *the post office (PO) on the southern corner of First Street untouched while buildings around it were demolished including the Oddfellow building across the street west of the PO – on the most south-western part of the UR area.*
- *the fire station remained as the Powers/Thompson block to the south of the fire station, and other buildings and houses to the North were all razed.*
- *the Oneida National Bank remained while the rest of the blocks south and west were razed.*

The question therefor is why were these buildings spared by the UR wrecking ball? Perhaps a topic for another day.

Things that make you go Hmmmmm!

Ilion, My Childhood, My Memories

i

Dedication

This book is dedicated to my parents:
Mary May Martin Hall Ludlow & Arthur William Hall

May you know the learning and joy you brought to me while I was growing up.

Hopefully I made you laugh, made you think, and made you proud.

And may your souls rest in peace.

Until we meet again, your loving son, Kevin.

Arthur William Hall 1923 – 1976
Mary May Martin Hall Ludlow 1927 – 2019
Armory Cemetery, Ilion NY

Acknowledgement

Many of the 100+ pictures included on the cover and within this book's pages, and some of the corresponding content, have come from sources such as:

a. The Ilion Public Library Historical Room

b. Ilionalumni.com

c. http://herkimer.nygenweb.net/ilion.html   Ilion History and The CENTENNIAL BOOK - "ILION 1852 - 1952"

d. The Internet Facebook groups "Ilion Rembers" and "Ilion Remembers"

e. Newspapers: The Ilion Sèntinel and the Evening Telegram

f. Https://en.wikipedia.org/wiki/Ilion,_New_York

g. The website of Http://Ilion.faithweb.com/photo.html (the Joe Smith collection which contains a large collection of pictures of old Ilion),

h. Https://nyheritage.org/collections/ilion-urban-renewal-collection

i. Ilion Yearbook Collection | New York Heritage (nyheritage.org)

j. Joseph Collea's photo collection, and his book: ***Our Town: Ilion, New York   A selective look at 300 years of history***

k. Dimitra Doukas book: ***Worked Over   The corporate sabotage of an American community***

l. And the authors personal photo collection

Special thanks go to Mike Disotelle, Historian, Ilion Free Public Library for his assistance in the research and gathering of the needed pictures and information that are included within this book. Special thanks also to Joe Collea for his advice and counsel as I meandered through the process of publication.

Knowing your history can give you the tools to shape your future. – Gloria Feldt

Ilion, My Childhood, My Memories

Index

Preface

My grandkids have asked me on more than one occasion –
"what was grandpa like as a kid?". And though I truly want to
answer that question for them, it is that question that had me
thinking of what in the way of a personal legacy did I want to
leave my family.

Therefore, I have written this book for the purpose of not only
answering my grandchildren's question of what grandpa was like
as a kid, but perhaps too, leaving behind a "trinket" to be shared:

- amongst people who may have had similar experiences.
- with those who may be fellow Ilionite's who have lived and walked
  the streets of old Ilion.
- with those who perhaps grew up in a town similar to old Ilion, a town
  that for the most part everyone knew, helped and watched out for
  other townsfolks.
- with folks who want to relive a simpler time in their life, a time of
  being a kid, running free, playing games in the street, and swimming
  in neighborhood pools, or nearby creeks.

Though it has been 50+ years since I walked those old Ilion
streets, I still recall many vivid memories of traveling around
town and going to the old downtown stores. It is these memories
and more that I speak about within the pages of this book, in the
hopes of giving my grandkids, and readers alike, a glimpse of my
childhood and a visit/revisit to a by-gone era.

We are here for but a blink of an eye, and we all work towards
fulfilling life dreams and ambitions. But what in the way of our

passing do we leave behind for future generations to know, to understand, to remember? It is my hope that this "trinket" will provide for an understanding of what it may have been like in Ilion for a young child during the 1960's.

Ilion has gone through a lot of changes in my lifetime, some good, and some maybe not so good. And it's through the telling of growing up in Ilion, the Ilion of mostly pre-urban renewal timeframe, that I will recall through the telling of my own childhood story.

Therefore, the goal of this book is meant to achieve the answering of my grandkid's question first, but to also impress upon them the message of remembering their past and to use it as perhaps an anchor of sorts with which to venture out from, while keeping themselves grounded.

I hope you all enjoy the reading of this book, and for my fellow Ilionite's I truly hope my story telling enables you to recall many of your own fond memories. And perhaps to assist you in that endeavor, the many pictures from that by-gone era that I have included to accompany my story, might just trigger some of your own fabulous memories.

Who knows, maybe you too will decide to have a sit down, grab the old PC and word processor, or failing that, grab a pen and paper and with those memories in hand, write your own "trinket" to leave behind.

Introduction

Ilion, My Childhood, My Memories is a book containing the many colorful antics of a young boy – who is me. A boy curious with the life around him, enjoying the many moments with his family and friends in his hometown of Ilion, New York.

Follow this young boy from his ages of 6 through 13, as he explores his home town of Ilion, the town he grew up in, the neighborhoods he lived in, and the many friends he enjoyed spending time with. Enjoy his many adventures and the sometimes-unexpected consequences of those adventures, not always anticipated by the young boy.

Explore too, how the town physically changed as the boy grew into a teenager and would eventually leave, moving to another state and leaving behind all that was familiar – his home, his friends, his school, his young life.

Memory is the treasure house of the mind wherein the monuments thereof are kept and preserved. – Thomas Fuller

Hopefully this fun read will bring to mind your own childhood memories and the enjoyable times of your youth.

My Christmas Closet Caper

One of my earliest memories is when I was around 6 or 7 and living in North Ilion on West River Street.   A typically quiet neighborhood just off of Central Ave, a major street through the town. I can remember one cold winter, near Christmas time, and I was doing what any curious child would do at that time of the year, I was looking for where my parents had hidden our Christmas gifts. I was at that age where I still wanted to believe in the magic of Christmas eve, jolly ole Santa bringing the gifts, but also wrestling in my head the logic of flying reindeer, toymaking elves and a sleigh full of toys for all the world's children.

My parents were not yet home from work so I thought I'd snoop around a bit and the first place I thought to look was in their bedroom. Typically, my parents would hide gifts (birthday etc.) in their bedroom as we were forbidden to go in there unless they had sent us for something specific. I decided to look in their bedroom and particularly I began my search looking around inside of their closet, which was a walk-in with a door. There was a window in the closet that was letting in light and though the room had a dark door and floor, I was able to see enough without turning on any other light.

I searched around the closet for a little bit, being ever so careful not to disturb the contents too much, but I was not able to locate any gifts. My conclusion was that either they had hidden the gifts in another location – or worse yet they hadn't bought any. However, while looking around I had noticed a crack in the window's glass, and being the curious child, I examined it closer. However, in my touching of the cracked window, I caused a piece of glass to come out and land on the snow that had fallen on the shed roof outside their window.

Being scared at this point, I knew what I had to do and that was to get the glass back and try to replace it into the opening in the window. I proceeded to open the window and step out onto the roof. It was slippery but if I took my time, I could retrieve the glass piece and put it back. I didn't have a coat on, only my day-time clothes and my shoes. It was very cold but I was inching forward slowly and was close to reaching the glass. A little bit more, but no luck as I was sliding down the roof and so was the glass.

The glass slid off the roof first, followed by myself. I landed close to the glass, and I was very fortunate that the glass did not break. Feeling both cold and some relief that neither the glass nor myself were harmed, I now needed to get back inside and get that glass back in place. My time was limited as my parents would be home soon, so I picked myself up, grabbed the piece of glass, and made my way back into the house through the back door.

Finding my way back upstairs to their bedroom closet and to the window, I managed to put the glass piece back in place. However, the glass just did not look right in the window, it just wasn't perfect enough to fool my parents. Maybe if I tweaked it just a bit it would look better, so I touched it again and you guessed it, it fell back out onto the roof and slid down to the ground. Oh crap, I now needed to work fast and get that piece of glass, make sure it wasn't broken, and put it back in the window.

Going back outside, I retrieved the glass and went back into the house. Once again, I went upstairs to my parents' bedroom closet and put the glass back in the window. This time when I replaced the glass, I did not care if it looked perfect as long as it stayed in the window, which it did.

For the rest of the evening, I was worried, and a bit scared, that somehow my parents would find out and I would be in terrible trouble, and would have to admit why I was in their bedroom closet. But if by some small miracle this all blew over, one thing was for sure, I was done looking for Christmas gifts that year. Feeling guilty for what I had done I worried as to how I could fix it and stop feeling this guilt. This bothered me for a few days, and somehow, I knew I had to make it right.

Ilion was a small town and after school I would sometimes walk-through downtown on my way home, not exactly a straight line from the grade school to our house. I especially enjoyed the walk through the town at this time of year, seeing the Christmas decorations in the store windows and the garland and lights that the town had put on display, hanging from the overhead wires. This was very picturesque to me, more of a Norman Rockwell setting, at least for a little kid. I also wondered how they got the lights onto the overhead wires. I was always curious in that way, noticing things, as my parents would say, things that at that age I shouldn't be worried about. Well, you know what they say about curiosity – good thing though – I'm not a cat!

Main Street Ilion, NY looking East

The main street in downtown Ilion was lined with stores on both sides of the street. Many of the old named store chains such as WT Grant, National Auto and the like, as well as local stores such as Wagner's Shoes, Powers News,

Ilion, My Childhood, My Memories

3

The Hungry 'I', and the local pet store. Do Do's Tropical Fish and Pet Supplies I believe was the name, a store that I would later come to know very well. However, that is a story for a bit later in this book.

The street was wintery in appearance, the grayish winter sky, the snow in mounds on the edge of the sidewalks in front of the stores, slush in the streets, and cars. The car tires, as they drove by making that slop-slop-slop noise through the slush, and the car tailpipes spewing the white vapor trail with the slight smell of unburnt gasoline. The occasional honk of the horns, the time and temp on the bank display, the lights from the Christmas decorations shining from store windows, and the people wearing buckled up boots, partially unbuckled near the top of the boot, scurrying about carrying their packages, with the occasional viewing of their breath in the air, all reminding me of the Christmas season.

"Christmas is a season not only of rejoicing but of reflection." — Winston Churchill

During my walk around town, I ventured into a couple of stores, one of which was the WT Grant store. I was looking around, just sort of window shopping, not knowing what I was looking for, but getting warm in the meantime. I meandered up and down the aisles, looking at many of the knick-knacks and losing track of time. Having gone around the isles a few times before finally spotting something, a paper-card like display cut-out of Jesus and the manger surrounded by Mary and Joseph, and the animals. This was the type of display you might have bought to put in a Christmas Card, or take to your office to put on your desk, or even stick onto one of the branches of the Christmas tree. For some reason I took a real liking to it and looking at the cost, I realized that I had enough change to buy it.

Taking it home I gave it to my parents, and putting it together (tab A into slot B) we displayed it on the end table near the couch. I would look at it daily and it gave me a happy feeling, a peaceful feeling, a more grown-up feeling. I'm not sure if giving it to my parents was my way of making up for not telling them what I had done, or a way to relieve my guilt of both snooping in their bedroom closet and knocking the broken piece of glass out of the window; but I knew that in giving it to them that I felt a calmness I had not felt in days.

To this day I do not know if my parents ever knew about the closet window incident or not. One thing is for sure, I never told them.

Writing this memory now during Christmas time 2021, brings to mind perhaps the real reason this display brought about calmness then. A reason that a curious 6- or 7-year-old little boy could not fully grasp. A reason that is the real reason for the season!

"When we recall Christmas past, we usually find that the simplest things—not the great occasions—give off the greatest glow of happiness." — Bob Hope

Another quick story about living at West River Street is my tree climbing adventure story. I was a bit of an explorer as a kid. There wasn't much that I wouldn't attempt, fearless of most things as I think little boys tend to be. After all, I fell off the shed roof and did not get hurt, so what could happen – right!

One day I was out in my backyard playing and basically exploring around. I saw the tree in the yard and decided that it would be a great idea to climb it. The lowest branch was not quite low enough for me to grab onto even with jumping to reach it. I looked around and found some items that when I stacked them, I was able to climb up onto the lowest branch.

I began climbing the tree, getting ever higher into the branches. I can remember looking around the back yard, looking into my neighbors' yard and just enjoying the views from high in the tree.

As I was looking around, I heard a voice say something about that I needed to be careful and perhaps I should get down from there before I get hurt. I looked around and saw that it was my neighbor standing near the fence that ran between our yards, and he was warning me to be careful and not get hurt.

Well, I was enjoying myself and not having any of his 'poking his nose into my business' and I promptly said – "My Tree, My Yard – I can do what I want". And with that the man left the fence and went back into his house. Now that's telling him…or so I thought.

Well, that's where the story takes a slight twist – or for such a little boy, a major twist. For you see the man next door had mentioned the incident to my parents, after all he was just looking out for my safety. Well, my mom was furious at me over this and first she lectured me about how children talk to adults and the respect we should show them. Then she made me take a wash cloth, clean off my face and hands and march my little back side over to the neighbors and apologize.

As a child of six I was really scared as I had not had to do anything like this before. I was not even sure how to do it or even what to say. I do remember walking over to the neighbor's house, washcloth still in hand and ringing his doorbell.

When the neighbor answered the door, and with my head bowing towards the ground, I managed to muster the words that I was sorry for what I had said. I do recall him saying that it was OK and that he was worried for my safety. I don't recall much after that except that I went home, feeling somewhat relieved that the incident was over – except my mom was waiting for me to come back and she continued her scolding for what I had done and asked what I had learned by the whole incident.

When I was older, Mom loved to tell that story and how she made me go over and apologize and my kids have heard that story probably a dozen times over the years. I sure do hope this is the last time it's being told.

"If you need a bit of perspective, climb a tree." – Pooh Bear

11 Benedict Ave and one Special Christmas

Our family moved around to different locations within Ilion a few times while I was growing up. We moved from Spring Street to View Terrace, and then to West River Street; and now the move from West River Street found us living at 11 Benedict Ave. And it would not be our last house move in Ilion!

Benedict Ave was off of Otsego Street across from the Masonic Temple and the statue, which was at the corner of Morgan and Otsego Streets. I remember I could look out of my bedroom window and look across the street at the Civil War Statue, called the Silent Sentinel, that was on a little grassy island, originally called Monument Park, in front of the Temple. A constant reminder that what is 'of value and moral' should not be lost to temptation, but defended against those that would deny it, or in any other way destroy it.

'Silent Sentinel' statues manufactured to represent the common soldier, were mass-produced following the Civil War. They can be found on hometown memorials in more than 30 states today. It represents the people who didn't come back or who did come back very much worse for the wear. All those soldier monuments — North and South — are a collective symbol of those losses from the Civil War that were felt in virtually every community throughout the country. A memorial meant to inspire as well as ensuring we never forget what was endured, scarified and lost by so many in a war between the North and South, Union vs. Confederacy and 'brother vs. brother', with the United States of America.

Monument Park changed overtime, as the original park had the monument flanked by cannons, had a sitting bench and flower/plant urns. The much larger setting also contained numerous shade trees.

Silent Sentinel, Morgan and Otsego Street, Ilion NY

What I did not know then, as a child, was that my Great-Great Grandfather –
Isaac Hall, fought in the Civil War and wrote a post-Civil War book titled:
History of the Ninety-Seventh Regiment, New York Volunteers: ("Conkling
Rifles") in the War for the Union. In reading excerpts from his book – later in
life, I learned that Isaac Hall and his regiment fought in many battles during
the war including Gettysburg, Appomattox, Antietam, and several others.
Additionally, my Great-Great Grandfather dedicated the 97th Regiment
Monument on July 1, 1889, in a ceremony held at the monument site in
Gettysburg.

As of this writing, the information I have about Isaac Hall is that he was a
Captain in the 97th Regiment, and he may or may not have lost an arm during
the war. Later pictures of him at a subsequent 97th Regiment reunion show
him with both arms, but it is not known if he had use of both arms.

"It was not well to drive men into final corners; at those
moments they could all develop teeth and claws."
— Stephen Crane, The Red Badge of Courage

97TH NEW YORK INFANTRY.

On Seminary Ridge, looking west. Ground over which Iverson's, Ramseur's, and O'Neal's (Confederate) Brigades moved in their opening attack on the first day.

A reminder of those that had fought to end slavery, and those that lost their lives in the battle.

The house on Benedict Ave was nothing really special architecturally, but I do remember it having sliding pocket doors. I also remember that it sat up the hill a bit and had a capped retaining wall about three foot high at the street level, bordering the sidewalk along Otsego Street.

One of my more vivid memories is that we would throw snowballs down into the street and sometimes at the cars as they drove by, down Otsego Street passing in front of our house. One day a snowball I threw actually hit a passing car on the side window. The driver screeched to a halt, got out of his car, and looking around he saw where the snowball had hit his car, and immediately knew the direction it had come from.

Being afraid as to what could happen next, I ran up the hill behind the house and into the woods. I hid there and watched as the man climbed the retaining wall and came into the yard looking around to see who could have thrown the snowball. He was upset and I could hear him mumbling, though I could not really hear what he was saying. Not finding anyone, he left shortly thereafter, and I retreated back down the hill and into my house.

Another memory was of walking to the Capitol movie theater, located on Otsego Street, during the holidays and seeing the movie 'Santa Claus Conquers the Martians'. Though I cannot remember if I was living in the Benedict Ave house at this time, the time of the movie release was in 1964, so I could have very much been living there.

The cost of the movie was probably a quarter, but mom and dad had given me fifty cents in order to get in and maybe buy some popcorn. This was the daytime matinee movie, and afterwards the movie theater manager handed out boxes of ribbon candy as you left the theater. The boxes were the size of animal cracker boxes that kids would have for snacks and I was very excited to have received it.

I remember going home afterwards and making the candy available for the family to share. Again, feeling grown up in doing this as it gave me an extra special feeling during the holidays to be able to share.

Santa Claus Conquers the Martians is a 1964 American science fiction comedy film directed by Nicholas Webster

Side story, next to the movie theater, at street level, was a doorway, and when you entered it there were a set of stairs leading to the second floor.

Ilion, My Childhood, My Memories
13

On the second floor was a hallway with several doors. The smell in the hallway was that of old shellacked wood. The floors were all wood boards and creaked a bit when you walked upon them. The doors were the type of door that had wood on the bottom of door and a glass window on the top. The glass was typically frosted and had lettering was on the outside stating the business office name.

One of those doors led you into a barber shop. It is at this barber shop where my dad would take us boys and where we would all get our haircuts at the same time. The barber was thin in appearance, I believe his name was Mr. Gordon Waterbury, and the shop itself as I recall had only one barber chair. Attached to the chair was a fairly long leather strap that Mr. Waterbury used to sharpen his straight razor upon, though as kids we never experienced the shave from that razor.

Being the smallest, I was usually first to get the haircut and they would put a board across the chair arms to elevate me as I sat upon it. And it was there that we would all get the same style haircut – a flat top. My dad always got the same flat top haircut and I think he probably had it cut that way since the time he was in the military (having served 2 years and deployed to the Pacific West Theater as part of the ordinance company of the tank division).

My dad in Pacific during WW2

Once seated in the chair the barber would drape his cape-covering over us, from around the neck, tied in the back, over the shoulders and hanging down the front covering past our knees, doing so to keep the hair off our clothes while he cut it. He then would spritz our hair with a little water, pull out his shiny large metal Flat Top Guide Comb, slide it through our hair, and lay the comb upon the top of our head. Then he would take his clippers and run it across the top of the metal comb, cutting away any hair that stuck above the comb. He would repeat this process as needed in order to cut all the hair to the same length.

Flat top Guide Comb

Afterwards he would trim the sides and back of our heads and trim around the ears. When that part was done, he would take a little gel, rub it in his hands and then run his hands through our hair standing the hair straight up as he went through it. Finally, he would take a comb and raise up the very front of our hair above our forehead, such that when he was finished it would look like we had the traditional standing flattop haircut.

Once that was done, he would take off the cape covering, brush off any loose remaining hair and then apply a little powder around the neck area at the top of your shirt collar. Then your haircut was complete and you hopped out of the chair for the next brother to get in. And finally, when all of us kids had our turn, then it was my dad's turn for his haircut.

One particular Christmas Eve, while living at Benedict Ave, the snow began to fall and continued falling throughout the night and into the next morning (according to the Utica Daily Press it was 1962). We must have had a foot or more on the ground by the time the snow stopped falling. This truly was a white Christmas – a real winter wonderland. The house phone started to ring early that morning and it was people calling who needed to get to Church or go visit their family or friends. They were asking for my older brothers, Art (we called him Butch) and Lon, to see if they would be willing to come and help them out by shoveling their driveways.

My brothers were up and out the door very early, dressed in appropriate attire, shovels in hand. They were in for a long day of hard work and we would wait for their return home before we opened presents and ate our Christmas meal. This waiting was taking too long for me, especially with presents to be opened, and I remember impatiently watching out the front window for Butch and Lon's return.

Finally, after what seemed like an eternity to me, my brothers returned, exhausted, cold, but very excited having shoveled out many driveways and sidewalks for several neighbors. After getting their snow clothes off, for the next several minutes my brothers pulled wads of cash, both bills and coins, from their pockets, and placed it on the table to count. Some of it still wet from the snow that had gotten into their pockets while shoveling. For me it looked like hundreds of dollars, more money than I had ever seen before.

My brothers were very happy indeed, tired too, but mostly excited at the money they had earned helping out the neighbors. I'm sure they both were thinking of all of the things they could buy with that money. What I tend to remember is that the final sum may have been 60 or 80 dollars, certainly a very tidy amount of money for pre-teen/teen school kids in the mid 1960's.

It is the things we work the hardest for that will reward us the most - anonymous

Additionally, I remember my brothers were also given several gifts, such as a radio, a box of candy, cookies and other miscellaneous treats with which to thank them for coming out to help. Gifts that were given in the spirit of the season for work done on Christmas day, helping out neighbors who were stuck in the snow. Needless to say, we were all excited now that my brothers were home and it was time to relax in front of the Christmas tree and open some presents.

There were not a lot of presents as I recall, but I do remember receiving a remote-control car and maybe some clothes. The car was red, about a foot in length, and was tethered to the control box with a black wire cord. The control box was also red with a 'T' shaped handle, and the battery was inside of the control box. The battery was a square 6v and almost the size of the control box.

There was a slight metallic smell as I raced the car around on the floor. The smell that often accompanied the use of train sets, race car sets and other mechanical toys of that era. I'm sure the smell came from the grease that was used on the gears of the car. That remote controlled car, which also came with pylons that could be set up making a pseudo course layout, kept me occupied for hours as I would race it around those pylons, on the wood floor of the enclosed front porch area of the house.

The remote-control car may have been my only present that year, I do not really recall. I do however, remember also asking for the Johnny Seven One Man Army gun, a toy gun which was advertised as seven guns in one. The

gun had a grenade launcher, a machine gun with tripod stand, and a detachable cap pistol, plus much more. My neighbor friend, whom I often played with, had one and I really liked it. But that toy was probably more expense than my parents could afford at the time.

The presents were all opened, the delicious meal consumed, and with nighttime upon us it was time to relax before going to bed. My brothers took their hard-earned money and the radio to our bedroom, as we all shared one bedroom. The radio was played for a little while that night and I remember hearing it play some songs as I drifted off to sleep, content with the days event, and I'm sure – anxious to play with my car the next day.

Ilion, My Childhood, My Memories

Parades, Paint Night and a Swimming pool

Living at 11 Benedict Ave proved an interesting vantage point for many town events. At times, parades (Memorial Day, Flag Day, Halloween, etc.) would pass by the house and we would observe from both our front yard as well as from the large windows of our living room. By the early 70's the parades were not as common of an occurrence as they once were, and most were smaller in size and it was more common to see parades performed on the main street through town.

Otsego Street 1966 Memorial Day Parade in front of 11 Benedict Ave, source: Photographed by Dr. Theodore Carney, Ilion NY

Living on Benedict Ave afforded us yet another vantage point to watch a yearly high school graduation tradition called **Paint Night**. During Paint Night the graduating students would go around town and paint their names, and other things, on the town roadways and in theirs and friends' driveways. This had been a long-standing tradition, and continues as a looked-forward-to yearly graduating student event.

In front of our house on Benedict Ave was a retaining wall that bordered the front of the property and the town sidewalk that ran along Otsego Street. From our house, during Paint Night, we could view the graduates apply their artistry to the retaining wall, as it proved to be a great canvas and therefore was a prime location for the applying of graduates' signatures along with their other artistic works and messages. I recall too that at times, over the years, that wall would be repainted by the town maintenance crew, providing for a clean surface for the next years graduating class.

However, as in other instances, Paint Night had found its way onto many street surfaces providing for a bit of a mess if cars happened to run over it when the paint was not dry. This Paint Night was now expanding to too many other surfaces throughout the town, and it became a bit of a nuisance. The town held meetings regarding Paint Night and after much consideration an ordinance was passed that called a halt to the spreading of this particular graffiti paint in all locations except in the graduate's own driveway and on the road in front of their house, or in another person's driveway with their permission. A concession for sure, but at least affording for this yearly tradition to continue for all future graduates of Ilion High School.

Retaining wall on Otsego Street, heading south towards Benedict Ave. Showing the aftermath of Senior Paint Night, source: Joseph Collea's personal photo collection

Ilion, My Childhood, My Memories

Beyond parades and Paint Night, living at 11 Benedict Ave offered opportunity at times to view the many cars that traversed Otsego Street. And of course, the occasional, and thankfully rare, police, fire and emergency vehicles racing by with lights flashing and siren blaring. When warranted, this was often accompanied by the Town Whistle blowing out the code indicating the street location of the emergency.

As was always the case with the town whistle sounding, this would send us rushing through the house to gather the yearly published Fire Alarm code card, typically hanging in the kitchen. And while we counted the whistle blows, we then consulted the code card to deciphered the street location for the emergency vehicle destination. This was often followed by someone in the family, mainly my mom, or older sibling, calling a relative or friend living in that neighborhood to make sure everyone was all-right.

Side story: in April of 1966 the town whistle blew as the next emergency was in progress. This time it would be to a relative's house at 116 East North Street. The home of my grandpa and grandma, and my uncle, aunt and their four children. The smoke emanating from the house was spotted by a neighbor whom reported it and sent the fire department into action. This was a fire that gutted the downstairs apartment that my uncle's family occupied.

Luckily my uncle, whom was home at the time, managed to rescue his four-month-old daughter, and escaped the house meeting up with his other children, whom had been playing in the back yard, safe from the fire. My parents who were both working at the time, immediately  *responded upon hearing the news. And although I do not remember much about this event, I do remember my dad assisting with his parents needed house repairs where he could.*

ILION'S NEW FIRE ALARM CODE

3 — Mohawk Valley General Hospital (Private)
4 — West Hill School (Private)
5 — North Fourth Ave. & Montgomery St.
6 — James St. & North 3rd Ave.
7 — Rand St. & Second Ave.
8 — Third Ave. & Second St.
9 — South Fourth Ave. & Grove St.
1-2 — Elm & Fourth Sts.
1-3 — Grove & John Sts.
1-4 — Otsego & John Sts.
1-5 — Otsego & West Sts.
1-6 — Third & Morgan Sts.
1-7 — Ilion High School (Private)
1-8 — Otsego & Richfield Sts.
2-1 — Second & West Sts.
2-3 — Second & Otsego Sts.
2-4 — First & Union Sts.
2-5 — West Main & Morgan Sts.
2-6 — West North St. & Pleasant Ave.
2-7 — West Main St. & Weisbecker Hill
2-8 — Electric Light Plant
2-9 — Annunciation School (Private)
3-1 — West Clark & Grant Sts.
3-2 — West River St. (Opposite Freight House)
3-4 — Central Ave. & North St.
3-5 — Central Ave. & State St.
3-6 — Central Ave. & Spruce St.
3-7 — Sperry Rand, Plant 2 (Private)
3-8 — East River St.
3-9 — North Street School (Private)
4-1 — Otsego & Main Sts.
4-2 — Remington Arms (Private)
4-3 — East Main St. & Hoefler Ave.
4-5 — Highland Ave.
4-6 — High & Armory Sts.
4-7 — East Main & Orchard Sts.
5-1 — Sperry Rand, Plant 1 (Private)
5-2 — East Clark & Catherine Sts.
5-3 — East North & Cottage Sts.
5-4 — East Clark & East Sts.

5-6 — East River & Cottage Sts.
6-1 — McCann & Spring Sts.
6-2 — East Main St. & View Terrace
6-3 — East Main St. & Hakes Road
6-4 — Hess Ave.
6-5 — Beech St. & Maple Place
6-7 — Spring St.
1-2-3 — West Main St. & Barringer Road
1-2-4 — West Montgomery & Division Sts.
1-2-5 — Second St. & Sixth Ave.
1-2-6 — South Fourth Ave. & Center St.
1-2-7 — South Fifth Ave. & Charles St.
1-2-8 — West Main & Shull Sts.
1-2-9 — Vosburg & West Montgomery Sts.
1-3-2 — Bellevue Ave. & Tucker Ave.
1-3-4 — North Fifth Ave. & West Rand St.
1-3-5 — West Rand St. & Barringer Road
1-3-6 — Barringer Road & Concord St.
1-3-7 — Woodland Ave. & George St.
1-3-8 — Marshall Ave. & Wayne St.
1-3-9 — Harriet & Brook Sts.
2-1-3 — Barringer Road School (Private)
2-1-4 — South Fifth Ave. & Wilson St.
2-1-5 — East Frankfort School (Private)
2-1-6 — West Rand St. & Massachusetts Ave.
2-1-7 — Second St. Ext. & Pennsylvania Ave.
2-1-8 — South Fourth Ave. & Brook St.
2-3-4 — Central Fire Station (Emergency)
2-3-5 — East Frankfort
2-4-6 — Rescue Squad
2-4-7 — Forge Hill Estates (North)
2-4-8 — Forge Hill Estates (East)
2-4-9 — Forge Hill Estates (South)
2-5-1 — London Towers
3-1-2 — Buchanan St. & River Drive
3-1-4 — Columbia Parkway & Monroe St.
3-1-5 — Gordon Place & Elm St.
3-2-1 — Huyck Trucking
1 — Lineman's Call
2 — Fire Out

Ilion NY Fire code as of 1972.

Ilion, My Childhood, My Memories

Heading North from Benedict Ave, down Otsego Street and, at the time, just after the end of the retaining wall, was a set of stairs that would allow a walker to go from Otsego Street up the stairs and exit out onto Armory Street. I sometimes would walk these stairs to the top, then walk back along Armory Street to Benedict Ave, and then come back down the Benedict Ave hill to my house.

Across the street from our house to the south of Benedict Ave, was what at the time was called the Towpath (**See Appendix 1 Towpath – Old Remington Raceway**). This pathway allowed us to walk to the high school, and in the summer time, allowed us a shorter path to travel to the swimming pool, dubbed the 'Big Pool'.

Several times as a young kid, I would go to the little stream along the side of the towpath, and gather up tadpoles in a jar, and watch them as they matured through their various stages of growth. Providing they were still alive; I would release them back into the stream (as long as it hadn't dried up which sometimes happened).

As I understand it, the Towpath today is paved over and is lighted. A chain is stretched across the opening at the Benedict Ave entrance, with just enough opening left in it for pedestrians to navigate, but a definite blockage to cars. However, if there was an issue that required emergency vehicles to access the Towpath, that chain could be removed quickly enough by the emergency responders.

Over the summer time I would sometimes walk the towpath to the Ilion pool (the big pool as we called it), and one summer I even started swimming lessons there. The big pool was a replacement pool for the original South Ilion Pool that was located near the Ilion Gorge. In the late 1940's it had been determined that the South Ilion pool was too small to accommodate Ilion's needs, and it was old, unsanitary and not near the center of Ilion population.

After several local town meetings on the subject of building a new pool, one that was bigger and more centrally located, it was decided that a proposition should be brought to the people of Ilion for a vote, and on June 10, 1950 the town voted in favor of building the new pool.

The South Ilion pool permanently closed on September 4, 1951. The new Ilion pool was completed and readied for swimmers in 1952, with a dedication ceremony happening June 23, 1952. (**See Appendix 2: The Ilion Pool**)

I can remember splashing around in the pool with my friends, and also trying to jump off the diving board. I am not what you would call a strong swimmer, in fact pretty much the opposite. I have a major issue in water, *I sink*. It took a lot of effort for me to keep myself afloat, however I could hold my breath for a time and that enabled me to swim quite a distant underwater.

Ilion, My Childhood, My Memories

Ilion Pool – dubbed the 'Big Pool'

Not being a strong swimmer, whenever I used the diving board, I would essentially walk off the board, landing in the water and struggle to get to the nearest edge of the pool where I would then pull myself along the edge until I reached the nearest ladder to climb out. Eventually the lifeguard on duty seeing my struggles, suggested I stay beyond the rope (as seen in the picture) as it was shallower there going from 3 feet to 5 1/2 feet in depth at the rope.

Ilion Big Pool on a summer day. Source: Ilion Free Public Library

Side story: As I grew older and had a family of my own, we took a trip to Jamaica. A nice tropical island resort made for relaxing. While there, one of the days we all decided to go snorkeling. Hesitantly agreeing I

Ilion, My Childhood, My Memories

indulged, that is until a wave crashed over me and I got a mouth full of salt water. Once that happened, I then proceeded to swim as best as I could back to the boat that brought us, and that is where I remained until the rest of those snorkeling came back on board.

I mention that trip as the ocean we swam in, being obviously salt water, was supposed to allow the swimmer to float more easily – giving you buoyancy. However, once again, as my family will attest, as they effortlessly floated – I Sank!

I'm not really sure why but in some ways, I miss that house on Benedict Ave. Maybe because of that Christmas morning, maybe because of the remote-control car, maybe because of my childhood past. Maybe too I miss that house because of its location in town. Whatever it is, I have the memories of that one special Christmas day to relive whenever I want.

I am glad, however, for my parents next house choice and its location at 73 North Fourth Ave; the new friends I will have, the new grade school I will attend – West Hill Elementary, and the many new adventures waiting for me.

West Hill Elementary School off Second Street Hill at corner of North Fourth Ave.

Living at 73 North Fourth Ave

We moved from Benedict Ave to North Fourth Ave the summer of 1966. My parents had discussed how they had bought the house on a type of bank note enabling them for home ownership. Later I would learn that it really meant that when the time came to sell the house, if the house did not sell, it would resort back to bank ownership and that my parents would be free and clear of the house, no more debt, but none of the profits either upon the future sale of the home. I was now nine years old, not really sure what all of that high financing house stuff was about, but I was looking forward to what adventures lie ahead in the new house, new neighborhood, new school and new friends.

Prior to moving in, my parents had spent evenings and weekends prepping the new house. Paint, paper, cosmetics, that sort of thing, along with some needed construction. The house was pretty much an empty shell waiting for some family to put their touches on it and calling it their own. My parents, again not having much in the way of finances, bought what they could afford, a true real fixer–upper (before it was 'Chic' to do so)!

The house was a three-bedroom, one bath home with a backyard, shared driveway and stand-alone garage. The basement was a combination stone wall with part dirt floor and part cement floor. This meant that over the years there would be much work to do in making the house our own. This also meant sharing a bedroom with my brothers for many more years.

When my parents had completed enough work readying the house to move in, they arranged for the move; us kids doing what we could such as packing up items in our room, or helping them load the car and borrowed truck. The move took a few trips from the Benedict Ave house, but with all the help we had, we were able to get it done in one day. We had just enough time to set up the bedrooms, and unpack enough of our belongings to give us the required accoutrements to accomplish the basic hygiene needed and enable meal preparation. Over the next few weeks, we slowly unpacked, emptying the packed boxes and finding places to put those belongings away in the new house.

The furnace in the house was an old Octopus type, very large with several large round ducts coming from it and going to the various room registers. As a side note several of these registers were in the floor and that enabled us to stand on top of them in the cold winter days; warmth from the heat flowing under our bathrobes as we stood there. But I digress.

Over the years my parents would make several changes to the house and at times I would be there working alongside my dad, watching, observing and learning. Mostly trying to stay out of trouble, but still being somewhat helpful for a 9- or 10-year-old.

My parents would over time, remodel the bathroom, the living room and den floors, adding on an addition to the kitchen and then remodeling the full kitchen, taking down the chimney that went from basement to the attic, putting in a new furnace and adding a side entrance to the house, one that also enabled access to the basement.

During the remodeling, besides the typical plaster and lath debris that when taken down sent dust throughout the house, there were moldings, door and window trim to deal with. Nothing re-useable was thrown away, instead it was labeled and taken into the basement, stored until needed again to finish the remodeling of a room.

When we were performing the house remodel, often we would find old coins in the wall. This is a known past tradition (or superstition) that by placing coins in the walls, concrete slabs, or in door jams was a way to bring good luck to the home owners. One such coin we discovered was a German coin, found when we were refinishing the floor in the den, and the sandpaper on the floor sander drum caught something and flung it across the room making a clank sound when it hit the opposite wall. My dad stopped the floor sander and investigated and found the coin, in almost perfect condition except for where the sander had caught hold of it.

The coin was the first of many found in and around the house. I personally found several more, especially in the front yard. For you see one of my jobs, and not really one I liked, was to rake the yard. I did that periodically and often would uncover a coin or two as I raked. Many of those coins were Indian Head penny's and I still have them in my collection today. I wish I had a metal detector back then to see what other coins I could have found around the yard and neighborhood. Finding the coins while raking the yard did make the job a bit easier and definitely more interesting.

> ### *There comes a time in every rightly constructed boy's life that he has a raging desire to go somewhere and dig for hidden treasure. – Mark Twain*

Living in a bedroom with 3 brothers was not all that bad, but not exactly a pleasant place to be on Chili dinner night. Sometimes we would chat about things and sometimes we would laugh and make noise to the point that one of our parents would yell to us to quiet down.

The room had a set of bunk beds and two stand-alone beds. I believe I had one of the bunk beds. Besides the beds we also had a couple of desks, one being a small roll top desk that somehow was mine. The desk had several drawers in it, some cubbies, and a roll

top that closed up and used a key to lock/unlock.

Whenever I made some money or perhaps did not eat lunch at school and saved that money, I would put it in the top drawer of the desk, and of course I'd lock up the desk. I kept that money secret from my brothers, as being older they were into things like record collecting, hanging out at the corner store and of course somehow buying the occasional pack of cigarettes to smoke with their friends – trying to look cool.

My brothers weren't really worried about having the smell of smoke on them and their clothes, as smoking then was pretty much ubiquitous. My dad smoked all the time and my mom did too but only on occasion. Pretty much our house smelled of smoke most of the time, and frankly we all became use to it.

Needless to say, I did not want them taking my money, money I had earned or somehow saved for something I wanted to buy sometime in the future. Even back then one of my desires was to eventually become wealthy enough to buy the things I wanted, and I somehow knew it took savings to get there.

One day my dad, prior to going to work, came into our room and asked if anyone had any money he could borrow, as he was looking for money to buy his lunch at work. My brothers each said that they did not have any and as my dad turned to leave the room, remembering the money I had in my desk drawer I asked him how much he needed.

He looked at me and said something like where did you get money, or some such thing. I remember something being asked along those lines as I told him

I had been saving it from odd jobs, and from not buying my lunch at school, instead saving that money too.

Upon opening the top drawer of my desk, my dad saw that I had several coins in there, dimes, quarters, nickels and pennies. My dad reached his hand into the drawer and began extracting the change, but at the same time he was lecturing me on the need to eat my lunch at school, and the nutrition it provides. Anyway, I half listened to his talk, all the while watching my savings vanish into my dad's pants pocket. I was happy that I was able to help my dad out that day, but also a bit sad that my hard-earned savings was gone.

Living on North Fourth Ave afforded us close location to Klippel's and Champagne's market, and for an 8 – 12-year-old, these were necessary places to stop for candy, soda, sports cards and balsa wood airplanes! However, as it was not common in my family to receive a weekly allowance, this meant that in order to have spending money, I had to find a way to earn it.

Typical for myself and my friends at our age meant that besides any money we might have received from relatives as birthday gifts, or money that our grandparents might have given us, earning money meant mowing lawns in the summer, shoveling driveways in the winter, and delivering newspapers year-round. For myself that meant doing all three. I remember mowing lawns with my brothers, helping where I could, as well as shoveling snow in the winter, and then there was the delivering of the Sunday Newspaper called the Syracuse Herald.

Mowing and shoveling snow meant hard physical work, and for the most part the customers paid us well and often would bring us cool drinks in the summer. In the winter, if we needed to shovel the snow from someone's driveway, and it was close to Christmas, the customer would often give us candy, or cookies too. However, there was always those few whom we would do the work for and would barely pay us anything. We learned quickly who those people were and avoided them.

I remember one such person – I won't mention his name, but he was a prominent real-estate person back in the day, and he had a very large driveway with plenty of parking space in the back of his property. After a heavy snow, my brother and I approached him to see if he wanted his driveway shoveled and he did. There was plenty of snow to shovel out of the driveway and because it was a large driveway, we had to carry each shovel full to the side of driveway to dump it, as it was too far to throw the snow. This took us several hours of shoveling, walking and throwing each shovel full to clear away the snow from this driveway.

Once we were finished, we went to the persons door to collect our money. My brother and I were thinking that this might be a job paying three or more dollars for each of us, but instead we received a total of three dollars to split. A small sum indeed for such a large driveway to shovel. We never approached that particular shoveling job again as we realized we would have made more money shoveling a couple smaller driveways as compared to shoveling his. An early lesson taught to me about the value of the time and money equation.

My older brother, Lon, also had a newspaper route for Sunday mornings, delivering the Syracuse Herald, a very thick newspaper and one that had a lot of circulars. Early on Sunday morning the newspapers and the circulars bundles would be delivered to our front door and at around 4 AM my brother and I would roust from our beds, get dressed and go downstairs to grab the bundles. Next, we had to open the bundles and take the circulars and insert them into the newspapers. Once that was done, we would wrap a rubber band around the newspaper and ready our satchels with the stack of papers.

At around 5 AM we were ready to leave the house, rain or shine, to deliver the papers. Occasionally if it was real bad weather, my dad would take us in the car, which was a treat. For you see our territory of delivering the paper was several blocks from (East/West) about Third Ave, off of Second Street, to Barringer road and from (North/South) area of Weisbecker Hill to South Fifth

Baseball field. Quite a distance for my short legs, and I had to keep up with my older brother's walking gate, all the while shouldering the satchel of papers. This is where I learned to walk real fast in order to keep up, thinking all the time of the reward to be received upon collection time.

During the week we would pick a day to go and 'Collect' from our customers. Occasionally we might have to make a second trip to some customers as they may not have had the funds to pay us at the time that we were collecting. Many times, the customer not only gave us the money for the newspaper delivery that they owed, but would also give us a 'Tip'. At times we were surprised because the tip might have been substantial, and especially at holiday times the tips were numerous. Though it was tiring work, we did manage to make enough money for both of us to afford some desired items.

I remember one particular summer, many of my friends had gone to camps, or otherwise had events that limited our game playing time. Being that I did not have a basketball hoop at my house to use, and there were no friends to play catch with, I went to West Hill School to see if I could shoot hoops in the gym. Bart Shelley was the principal of West Hill, and was a very nice person, though when needed, he could be that disciplinarian and set you back on the straight and narrow. Mr. Shelley, as we referred to him, knew my parents well and most every Christmas my mom would bake batches of cookies, amongst which was one of her specialties called Cucidata, an Italian Fig filled cookie, and Mr. Shelley was always a recipient of one of mom's cookie trays.

Ilion, My Childhood, My Memories

Mr. Shelley allowed me to play in the gym, and around noon time took me to the school's cafeteria and gave me some ice cream – you might remember those ice cream cups we'd all get in the cafeteria at lunchtime, the ones with the wooden spoon attached. After enjoying the ice cream, I wound up that afternoon helping Mr. Shelley out with some things in the school, and at the end of the day he gave me a dodge ball and one dollar for my efforts. This was a great day for me, and given that my friends would be gone for a week or two, I thought that maybe I would go back to the school the next day to see if I could help them in any way.

Mr. Bart Shelley, Ilion Library Historical Room – Throwback Thursday

Mr. Shelley understood that my friends were gone for a time and he agreed to let me play in the school's gym and to also help out the school's custodian with his summer time work. This involved cleaning desks, mopping floors; and resupplying chalk, erasers, and books to the classrooms etc... Mostly readying the school for the start of classes in the fall. I worked right alongside with the custodian, stopping for breaks when he did, and of course each day at lunch time there was ice cream!!! Then at the end of each day I received my dollar. I felt rich for sure, and it made the time go by, and just as quickly my friends were back home and my time at West Hill School came to an end.

I can't recall where I spent the money or what I bought, but I imagine it was probably spent at Klippel's and Champagne's market, and the downtown stores of Do-Do's Pet's, Power's News, Bonn's Sports and W.T. Grants. All of the typical shopping places for me and my friends. And the items of purchase I'm sure were sodas, ice cream, sports cards, HO Scale race cars, tropical fish and supplies, balsa wood airplanes, squirt guns and 'caps' for our cap guns. All of the necessities to bring much joy and reward for my efforts!

Some last recollections from my years as a student at West Hill School, included gym class, and a class given by Mr. Joseph Tamburro. I had Mr. Tamburro as a teacher at West Hill School in the fourth grade. A very good teacher, and I found out quickly that you do not talk out of turn in his class as he was always armed with an eraser. I can recall it sailing by mine and other students' heads on a few occasions. He never hit anyone with the eraser, as he'd only throw warning shots. Not so surprisingly, no teacher would ever be able to do that today during class.

Gym class was another fun time for me, and I especially liked it when we played dodge ball. As I have mentioned I was a bit of a scrawny kid with not a lot of athletic skill, but in dodge ball I was one of the children picked quite early when team players were picked. The reason being I could catch the ball no matter how fast the ball was thrown. Another kid in the class, Mike Helmer, was also very good at dodge ball, and he could catch and throw the ball pretty hard too.

One of my fondest memories is playing dodge ball in the West Hill gym. There was this one game where I was on the same team as my neighbor Mike Helmer, a bigger and more muscular player than myself. Mike was a good friend and we had played many a street games growing up together on North Fourth Ave, playing baseball at South Fifth Ave, and trying out for one of our towns Little League teams.

This particular dodge ball game started quickly and was going fast and furious right from the start. Several of our team mates were eliminated quickly by the other team, as they had 6th graders who could really 'whip' the ball with surprising accuracy. It seemed to me at the time, as I recall, that the other team was eliminating our team players at a rate of twice that of our team eliminating their team players. Mike and I were holding our own with the back-and-forth action, and soon it came down to two players remaining on our team, just Mike and I. The other team had perhaps as many as eight players, but that would not last for long.

Being the smaller sized kid left for our team, I became the first target. The balls began to fly, and Mike and I managed to escape being hit. Soon another ball was thrown directly at me and I caught it, eliminating one player from the other team. Then a second ball came my way, I caught that too. I remember giving the balls to Mike to throw as he was the stronger thrower. And as I recall after a few minutes, it was down to Mike and I and two players on the other team. Those two players took turns targeting Mike and I. Again, back and forth it went and then one of the strongest players on the other team, a 6th grader, took aim at Mike. He whipped that ball real hard, and Mike, who had his back against the gym wall, readied himself and with a sounding smack Mike caught the ball as it hit him square in the chest. With that catch and the elimination of the other team player, Mike and I then took aim at the remaining player, eventually the ball meeting its target and eliminating him, giving our team the win! That was an exciting time for sure!

Dodgeball for the Love of the game!

For me these are fond childhood memories of a time that was simpler, a relaxed and more fun time, less complicated time, and in some ways a more regimented time of my life. As a child growing up in that era, and as an Ilionite, you knew what was expected of you, and you performed to the best of your ability. For us kids, the rewards then were our many friendships, school grades, athleticism, safety, and spending money – to name a few; and now as we are in our more senior years of life, we are still being rewarded by the gifts we have carried forward in the form of some of our fondest memories!

Memories are perhaps the best gifts of all – Gloria Gaither

Recently, my wife (Sharon) and I had lunch with my younger sister Diane and her husband Mike (Palinski). It was a good lunch and gave us plenty of time to talk of world events and such things.

As we were leaving, I gave my sister a copy of my first book **_My Christmas in Rosemount,_** as I had not shared it before then with her, or any other family member. She was delighted to receive it and later revealed that she began reading it on their drive back home, and as she said – laughing quite a bit.

Before we departed that day, she reminded me of two stories of our living on North Fourth Ave. The first story was that the first day of attending West Hill School, she and I walked to school and arrived earlier than any other student. We waited at the back door of the building for school to begin, and she remembers it was chilly that morning. We knocked on the door several times and eventually someone opened the school door and let us in, letting us stay in the boiler room, warm and secure until the start of the school day.

The second story was to do with our walk home from school. As she remembers there was one day that we were both walking home from school and she was being pestered by one of her classmates. To give you some perspective on our ages, I was probably 9 or 10 and Diane was 6 or 7.

The young boy pestering my sister appeared to want to kiss her, or some such thing that little boys are apt to do trying to express their liking of a girl. Well, it was apparent from the story she related, that as she remembers it, she did not want to have anything to do with that boy.

She reminded me of how I, watching out for my younger sister, got behind the boy and gave him a karate chop to the back of the neck, just above the shoulder – making a loud **HI-YA** sound as I did it. This supposedly scared the boy off and enabled us to walk the rest of the way home without being bothered anymore.

Memory is the treasure house of the mind wherein the monuments thereof are kept and preserved. – Thomas Fuller

I must admit, though as she related these stories, I did have recollection of that 'first day of school' story, even remembering the janitor that was there in the boiler room. However, the second story of the boy and the karate chop escaped me. Though it does sound plausible as something I would do, I'm going to have to take her word for it – for now.

Memory is the Diary we all carry about with us.
Oscar Wilde

A Boy, A Cub Scout, a Clown and Baseball

Somewhere around 9 or 10 years old I joined the cub scouts. I remember at one time our Den Mother was Mrs. Jeffries. Mrs. Jeffries, her son Jim and their family were next door neighbors of mine, and Jim and I were in the same grade. Usually you could find Mike, Jim, myself and others somewhere in the neighborhood, playing ball, riding bikes and the like.

My parents signed me up for cub scouts and I did enjoy it very much. We would have weekly meetings, talk about the scout oath, how to help our community, work on achieving badges, and plan for different outings.

Side story: Recently I ran across a posting in The Evening Telegram dated November 25, 1959 titled 'Cub Pack 7 Has New Cubmaster'. In the article it states that Harry Wright was named new Cubmaster and that Arthur Hall was named assistant cubmaster. Along with that, the article states that another Arthur Hall and two other boys were inducted as bobcats. My assumption being that the assistant cubmaster was my dad, and the inducted bobcat was my brother. I only wish that they both were alive to confirm my assumption.

I remember several kids in our grade school class also being part of the scout pack, as well as being members of the little league baseball team. In such a small town, by the time you reached middle school you pretty much knew all of your class mates, and had been to many of their life events such as graduations, weddings, and cook outs with them and their parents.

And of course, we had the public pool, big and little pools side by side. Many summers we would walk to the pool to swim, rough house a bit, and just hang out. We would meet up with many of our classmates and chat about who was liking whom, who might have broken an arm or got stitches, any kids moving away or moving into town, and what the next school year would be like. Small town banter to help fritter away the day and the summer.

Between house chores, swimming, riding bikes, baseball, hanging out and cub scouts – life was pretty full for a little tyke like me. Oh, and let's not forget that at the end of North Fourth Ave., a mere block and 1/2 from my house, was Klippel's convenient store. They had the typical bread, eggs, milk, ice cream and other grocery items, but they also had penny candy and a soda fountain counter. I spent many a penny in that store. It was also directly across the street from my grade school – West Hill Elementary, and as a student I would often accompany my school friends there after class.

I remember that they had a gum ball machine that had all different color gumballs. You put a penny into the slot on the side of the machine, then slide the lever and 3 or 4 gumballs would fall into the receiving tray. But there were a few special gumballs in the machine – those were the multi-colored spotted ones. If you were lucky enough to get one of those to drop into the tray, then you would take it to the register and 'turn it in' to the cashier person and they would give you a nickel. You could certainly buy a lot of penny candy for that.

One of the candies I would buy was Mallo Cups. They cost a nickel and so I did not get them very often. There was another reason besides taste that I liked to buy them. Inside of each Mallo Cup wrapper was Mallo Cup point

cards. Once you had collected '500 points' you could send them into the manufacturer and they would send you back a box of 10 Mallo Cups.

Most of the time when you unwrapped a Mallo Cup you would get a 1, 5 or 10 point card in the wrapper, but occasionally you could get a 25 or a 50 point card. And there were those rare times that you might find a 100-point card. I had heard rumors of a 500-point card, but I never saw one.

Overall, I managed to collect 500 points on a few occasions and sent it into the manufacturer to get my box of 10 Mallo Cups. I can remember waiting

Ilion, My Childhood, My Memories

and counting the days until I would receive them, rushing home to check the mailbox to see if the package had arrived. And on that day that they did arrive, it was a joyous time indeed eating Mallo Cups, sharing some, and just enjoying life.

Attending organized activities, playing organized sports, a pickup game in the streets or just hanging out – anytime I was with my friends was a great time, often a time that past by too quickly. Activities like Cub Scouts not only gave us more time to hang around, but there were many projects to complete in order to achieve your scouting merit badges.

I remember building things during our scout pack meetings using materials provided by the den mother. Often times too, there were treats at these meetings. But what I liked most was hanging with my friends and going on outings or 'Scout Trips' as we would call the.

Some of these outings including walking to the local library or to the local playground (around the corner), but there was one special outing that I remember and that was the trip to WKTV television station atop Smith Hill in Utica, for the afternoon live showing of **The Bozo Show**. And it would also mean that we would get out of school a little early to go. What fun it was going to be!

The following is taken from an article titled: About WKTV.

> *Of all the WKTV produced programs -- the best remembered was the daily after school show featuring the clown with the bright red hair...BOZO. Ed Whittaker was a staff announcer at WKTV when the station purchased the syndicated rights to the BOZO character and cartoons. Whittaker was a trained actor and the perfect choice as BOZO. Many weekday afternoons, Boy Scout packs and Girl Scout troops would make their way up Smith Hill to sit in the bleachers. The kids would watch BOZO cartoons, play games and they might get a hamburger from MacDonald's or a Hostess Cup Cake.*

Ilion, My Childhood, My Memories

There we all were, our full pack, sitting in those bleachers and watching the show. We sat through cartoons and had a snack and then it was about time to have the game. Bozo had several different games that he would choose some lucky boys or girls to play. And of course, the winner would get a nice prize and the runner up would also get a little something too.

There we were all waiting patiently to see what game was going to be played that day and who might be selected from the audience to participate. Then they rolled out the table and there it was, the ping pong game.

The object of the ping pong game was to have two players, each at opposite ends of the table. Bozo would then place a ping pong ball in the center of the table and when he said go, without using your hands, and only by blowing at the ball, you needed to get it past the player at the opposite end. You could not touch the ball with any part of your body, otherwise you would lose.

Next came the selection of the names. To select the names, a container was prepared containing paper slips with names of those in attendance printed on them. Bozo would draw pieces of paper from the container and then he would read aloud the name on the drawn paper, and that person would be the participant in the game. We were all excited with anticipation that we would have our name called and that we would have a chance to be crowned that day's winner of the game.

Bozo drew the first slip of paper and called the name, it was not my name, but we all clapped for the person chosen. That person would then be invited to go stand by Bozo and wait for the second name to be chosen. All of us now on the edge of our seats waiting to hear our name called, and Bozo pulled the next piece of paper and said the next person selected is…drum roll please…and… yes, he chose me – Kevin Hall!

I could not believe I was chosen, and boy was I excited. Not only was I on the Bozo show, but I was picked to take part in the game too! I was one very happy little boy, feeling on top of the world. But now would the happiness last

– was I good enough to defeat my opponent and win the big prize? Would I be capable of winning and being the scout pack hero?

To begin Bozo got us both positioned at our respective end of the table. I remember both the bright lights and the overhead microphone above the table. Then Bozo held the ping pong ball over the center of the table, asking us if we were ready, we both nodded yes and at that moment Bozo placed the ball into the center of the table.

We both began to blow hard at the ball, it barely began to move, but then the more we blew air at the ball the faster it moved. Back and forth it went, slow at first then gaining speed and getting faster and faster, our little hearts racing as the game went on. The ball was really moving fast and coming towards me, but I was able to deflect it away and send it flying back down the table.

My opponent was also able to deflect it back to me, and we continued this back and forth, the kids in the bleachers cheering us on as the game progressed. I remember hearing the cheers, the laughter, the 'oohs and aahs' as the ball was close to falling off the table but somehow, we managed to keep it going.

Back and forth and back and forth the ball went. I know I was getting a bit winded so I imagine my opponent was too. Then it happened, and with one powerful breath I sent the ball flying down the table towards my opponent. I remember thinking that this was it, it was going off his end this time. However, he had more wind in his sail then I did and he sent it flying back towards me, and I tried blowing hard at it, but not enough and off my end of the table the ball went. My opponent had succeeded and he was the winner!

There was lots of clapping and cheering from the bleachers and I remember Bozo bringing us both back to the center of the room, again standing next to him. He congratulated both of us and gave us our prizes. Though I do not recall what the winner's prize was, I remember mine was a kaleidoscope, and that I was happy to have received it.

That was a fun outing for sure and one that has given me much pleasure recounting the story to my children and grandchildren. My wife has heard that story a few times and without telling me, she decided to see if she could obtain a copy of that broadcast from WKTV.

She called WKTV and talked with the station manager. She told him of the story and what fun I had, and that she wanted to surprise me with a taping of the show, if it still existed. The station manager was very apologetic but unfortunately, as he told my wife, there are no tapes from that time frame of the station's history as the shows were not recorded then.

This was very disappointing to my wife, and when she told me what she had tried to do, I could feel her disappointment. I really do appreciate the effort she made, and just the thought that she would do that makes me feel very happy indeed.

I have my memories from that simpler time in my life. The memories of a little boy running and playing, doing chores, going to the store, riding his bike, playing ball, tag or hide and seek – and just hanging out with friends. Some of those childhood friends have passed away, most of them I have just lost contact with. But those memories of that time in my life, I will have forever.

Who's Bozo? Bozo the Clown, that's who Bozo is. When I was a kid, Bozo the Clown was the clown, bar none. – George Costanza SEINFELD Episode no. 84 "The Fire" (Original air date 5 May 1994)

Ilion, My Childhood, My Memories

43

One of the things a young boy typically did in the springtime, in our town of Ilion, was to join Little League Baseball, (at that time there were no 'T'-ball leagues). We did that not only to have fun and to be with friends, but also for the wanting to emulate our own major league hero's. And in doing so hopefully we would fulfill our own boyhood dream of catching that fly ball, smacking a home run, sliding into home plate and scoring the winning run. Dreams held by many in the youthful game of baseball.

The baseball teams were spread around the village and if you joined the Little League you were assigned to a team depending upon where you lived in town. As I recall the team names were the Tigers, Braves, Cardinals, and the Yankees, and for me living on North Fourth Ave, that meant that the team for our section of the town was called the Tigers.

There was an orderly process in making it onto a team, and the first point of order was for tryouts. Tryouts were held each year in early spring and due to the number of those trying out and their various skill levels, the league had its several baseball teams divided into A, B and C teams. Of course, most everyone tried out for the A team, but as try outs proceeded, each person was graded on skill level, and then each person was assigned to A, B or C team. I typically was assigned to the 'B' team. I could field and throw the ball fairly well, but my hitting was lacking in distance and I was not a real fast base runner. However, my ball handling ability enabled me to play on the B team with other commensurate skill level players.

It was always a bit of a letdown to see some of my friends make the 'A' team, and though I was happy for them, it for sure dampened my enthusiasm a bit. For you see we had a great ball player from Ilion that we all knew through word of mouth, or even having watched him play. He was someone that was destined for the major leagues and whom eventually played for the Cardinals – making his debut in 1969, and later traded to the Cubs, and then the Montreal Expos, and his name was Charles Frederick "Boots" Day.

I won't dwell upon Boots Day other than to mention that the kids of little league would think of him and his amazing talent on the ball field often with dreams of stardom in their own eyes. Dreams of the possibility of perhaps one day they too might make it to the Big Show…the Major Leagues! However, as was often the case the vast majority of the little leaguers would at best, go on to play high school ball and perhaps some of them might even go on to play college ball.

At the time that I was a little league player, besides Boots Day I was only aware of one other fellow Ilionite who played for the major league, that was my uncle – Doug Hall. In 1952, Doug was signed to the Brooklyn Dodgers. He had played with them for a short time before being drafted to the United States Army in November of 1952. After his discharge, again Doug played AAA baseball for two years with the Brooklyn Dodgers.

I also remember my dad played ball and was a member on a team sponsored by the place he worked at, I believe that sponsor was the Sperry Rand Corporation. I was young then and do not remember much detail, but my mom would often tell the story of how my dad broke his leg playing ball, it involved a slide into home – though I do not remember if my dad was doing the sliding or if he was the catcher at the time of the slide. However, his leg was broken and he was laid up for a while allowing it to mend.

As you can well imagine, someone like me with the family history of ball playing, I was going to try hard to earn my wings – so to speak, to make my mark and have my own heroic baseball stories to tell. However, trying my hardest, the best I could do was to make the 'B' team, and only rarely was I called up to the 'A' team.

The typical team practices were held weekly afterschool and the games were held mostly on weekends. Each practice night many kids would grab their ball caps and gloves, draping the glove over the handlebars of their bikes, and ride off to the team practice. During practice, after some warm up stretching exercises, we would pair off and toss the ball back and forth. Then one of the team coaches would take some of the kids for outfield practice, another coach would take kids for infield practice, and then a pitching coach would practice with the team pitchers. After all of that practicing, we would then do some hitting practice. All of this being done in order to get us ready for 'game day'.

Most often you would find me practicing with the infield group as I was a good utility man and could play second base, short stop or third base as needed. This is where my ball fielding and throwing was most utilized. Occasionally I might be called upon to play outfield, as again I could throw the ball pretty far, and though not often a need for that, it was appreciated when it was needed.

The difference between practice and the game day was four things – the location of the game playing field, the wearing of our baseball uniforms, parents in the bleachers, and after game snacks. Aside from that, many of us would still ride our bikes to the game field, which might be across town – where you would see probably 30+ bikes all parked along the fence area near one of the team dugouts. After parking your bike, and having all the players gathered together, the coach would give us a team 'pep-talk' to get us 'charged' and ready for the game.

I do not have much in the way of any really great game event to talk about, although I do recall one time while playing and I was coming up to bat with one person on base. The coach took me aside for a little pep talk and said that this was my time, he told me to give that ball all I had and give it a ride (meaning to give it a good hard smack).

As I recall I let the first pitch go by for a ball, then I let the second pitch go by – for a strike, and on the third pitch I gave it all I could and smacked that ball for a line drive, out of the infield going into center field and eventually rolling to the outfield fence. Even being a slow runner, I managed to turn the hit into a double and enabled the runner, who had been on first base, to score for an RBI (run batted in). I further recall, as I stood tall on second base, my coach looking in my direction with a big smile on his face giving me the thumbs up! I was pretty happy for sure. And for the most part, that was the highlight of my little league ball playing days.

Ilion Little League Baseball Field

Ilion Little League ball game, picture taken from the press box, photo courtesy of Mike Disotelle, Historian, Ilion Free Public Library

I did receive a trophy in 1969 as a member of the Tigers team, though I do not recall why. Where we the champs of the 'B' team, was our team in the top two, or did everyone on the team get a trophy (not a common occurrence then). I wish I knew more about it, but for now that part of the story is lost to history. However, I do have the trophy and some nice memories of a fun time of my life; just a 12-year-old boy enjoying the game of baseball with my friends in our town of Ilion.

Ilion Midget League,
69 Tigers,
K. Hall,
Oneida National Bank – Kiwanis

September 10, 1969

ILION'S 1969 MIDGET LEAGUE ALL STARS, left to right, row one, Brian Bruce, Tom Brayton, Ken Keddell, Kevin Fox, Tim Morris, Jim Gorman; Row two, Kevin Matthews, Tim Jock, Ken Farrington, Carl Scaparo, Richard Bohr, Harold Lewis, manager; Row three, Don Jordan, coach, Matt Soules, Dale Outtram, Larry Thibault, Mike Helmer, Ed Patterson, coach.

Ilion Midget League All Star Baseball team of 1969. Picture, courtesy of Dale Outtrim's posting in the 'Ilion Rembers' Facebook Website. The letter on their caps represented the little league team they played for i.e., B for Braves, C for Cardinals, T for Tigers and Y for Yankees.

The Big Christmas at North Fourth Ave

Very often we would play in the street outside of our house with several neighborhood friends. We would play baseball, whiffle ball, touch football, kickball and the like. The sport chosen to play would be determined by how many people were available at the time. Once sides were chosen, we would review the rules and make sure everyone was aware of the bases when the chosen sport dictated that bases were needed.

Whenever we played in the street we would always look out for cars. When a car was seen coming down the street, one or more people would yell **CAR**, and then we would move to the curb side of the road taking with us any bases we might have put in the street. Occasionally we would be fooled by the yell of **CAR**, as the particular car might make a last-minute turn into a driveway ahead of where we were actually playing in the road.

The typical group of neighbors who would most likely be present included, as I recall, the Eller's, the Helmer's, the Bechard's, the Jeffries's, the Janicki's and of course us – the Hall's. Though not all of these neighbors would be there for every street game, but when we all were present, we usually played touch football or kickball so that all people could play.

What I liked to play most when there were a lot of us, was kickball as we could all get a turn at kicking the ball. Sometimes when we played touch football, some of us smaller, younger kids just ran around but we really didn't get the football to make a play. This would upset me a bit but I really never had a voice in the matter.

We did not live on a real busy street, car wise, but during Monday to Friday we could rely on the cars coming down the road from around 4-5pm due to the workers getting home from their job. On Saturday and Sunday there was no real specific time that cars would come down the street. Regardless of the day however, you always had to keep an eye out for cars so that we could get off the road and allow the car(s) to pass.

When the fall and winter weather was upon us, we would still play in the street, only we might have warmer clothes, coats, hats and the like. We still played the typical games as we did in the summer time, and for the most part with the same rules in force. When there were high snowbanks on the curb of the road, and if it was touch football, we would allow the pushing of a player into a snow bank to stop them from scoring a touchdown. Lots of fun.

Occasionally a snowball fight would break out, and of course there was the snow fort building connecting forts from neighbor yard to neighbor yard in the mounds of snow that was pushed by the plow onto the yards. However, as was always with my family, the house chores would need to be done first before we were allowed to go out and play. No exceptions! And when the street lights came on, if we were still playing, we needed to end the game and go home. That rule pretty much applied to all of our neighborhood friends too.

It was December and winter was now upon us and there was snow on the ground – but not a lot. There was a light snow in the air, hopefully this would remain and enable us to have a white Christmas, not always something you could count on – but something I always wished for! And it was this year that our Christmas presents would be the largest ever. But with the amount of presents we would receive; I still wonder where my parents had hidden them.

There were a group of us out playing in the street. While playing, as usual, we would occasionally yell '**CAR**' and need to move to the curb. One time we yelled **CAR** and the car was a station wagon, and it was my parent's car. When it drove by, it did not go into our driveway, instead it went passed our house. When it passed, I noticed in the back window that a blanket was covering what I surmised were several boxes of different heights.

Many thoughts danced around in my head: why did my parents drive by, what were in those boxes, where were my parents going to, and on and on. This was not normal acting by my parents and when they finally returned to the house, there were no boxes in the station wagon. Being that this was Christmas time, all kinds of suspicions surrounded this action by my parents.

Soon we were off on school break for the holidays and quickly Christmas would be upon us. Our tree was set up and decorated, dressed in all the family ornaments. This year's tree was placed in the living room near one of the windows. My mom's ceramic decorated tree, which she had made at DeJohn's Ceramic class, had been put on the table by another window. Other small decorations adorned the dining room, but we had no outside lights or lawn displays of any kind.

My parents have never decorated the outside of the house with lights while I was living with them, at least not that I can remember. I'm really not sure why they didn't, but several of our neighbors did and I really appreciated that. Their houses just looked happier all lit up, especially with the snow falling outside.

Most years my parents would take us to see the neighborhood light displays, driving around various neighboring streets looking for the most decorated houses. Also, we would make a yearly drive to a neighboring town, maybe a half hour from our home, to see a very large Christmas display at Trinkaus Manor, that included lawn ornaments, lighted trees, large open story book lighted displays telling the story of the Night Before Christmas (as memory serves), Christmas music playing, and what fun that was. The line to view this display was often long and may take an hour or so to drive through the line and view the display.

We would slowly drive though, stopping ever so briefly at a display, our eyes wide with wonder. Some displays so amazing that it caused a shiver down your spine, or goosebumps on your arms. Row upon row of multi-colored twinkling lights, moving lawn displays, and many lights strewn through the trees, all making for one spectacular holiday display. The sites and the sounds ever increasing the feeling of Christmas and the wonder and magic of the season.

From 1955 through 1992 Trinkaus Manor hosted an annual Christmas light display featuring over 750,000 lights, drawing in thousands of visitors, until it was destroyed by fire in 1992.

Christmas eve was soon here and I was getting excited for the next day and our Christmas morning traditions! One tradition was that I was the 'Scout', elected by my older brothers to get out of bed and to sneak quietly down the stairs to get a peek at the presents and then report back to them what I saw.

Having our bedroom right next to mom and dads', as the scout I needed to be very quiet and make sure to not step on any squeaky floor boards of the hallway and stairs, or to do anything that might cause my parents to catch me in the act of sneaking downstairs.

Knowing that I was to be the scout again this year, when no one was around I practiced walking the hallway. Looking for the squeaky boards, memorizing their locations, and doing the same thing for the stairs. I was going to be as ready as I could be to fulfill my mission.

My scouting trip that morning was a success and boy did I have things to report to my brothers. First thing was that it was going to be really difficult leaving the stairs and going into the living room as the presents were stretched from the tree, on the opposite side of the room, all the way over to

 the stairs. There were presents everywhere, mountains of them. There were ride-on toys for my brother Randy, dolls with accessories for my sister Diane, hair fixings and beauty aids for my older sister Rosemary, toys and clothes for me and my older brothers Lon and Butch, and many more items – too many to count and too hard to remember them all.

Another of the family traditions was that my parents were to be the first ones up on Christmas morning and they would go down stairs, make a pot of coffee, and get ready to turn on the tree lights. For you see, none of us kids were allowed to get up from bed and go downstairs until the tree lights were turned on, and even then, we had to wait for our parents to say we could come on down and get the presents. (By the way, I carried on this tradition with my own children too).

My parents woke up shortly after my adventurous scouting trip, probably because they heard us boys chatting in the next room. They went down stairs and as I mentioned, they made a pot of coffee. When the coffee was ready, they went into the living room with their coffee cups, turned on the tree lights, and settling back in their easy chairs they would then call us all to get up. Needless to say, I was one of the first ones down the stairs.

The living room was one giant warehouse of presents, it took us what seemed like hours to open and look at them all. I'm still not sure how my parents afforded all those gifts, but I am glad they did. My parents never gift wrapped the toys as they would say, Santa does not wrap the presents he gives (well, I have watched the Christmas TV shows and Santa's gifts appeared to be wrapped to me), but this year was a bit different as some of the presents were indeed wrapped. However, I didn't care at all, as having some of the presents wrapped enhanced the anticipation of unwrapping the gift and discovering the toys and games we had received.

My memory of what I received that year is a bit foggy and I may be getting some of my gifts confused with other year's gifts. What I do remember, however, is the quantity of gifts all spread out throughout the living room, leaving little walking space, hearing the oohs and aahs and seeing the smiles on my siblings and parents faces as we opened and played with our gifts.

But I had to wonder why so many gifts when that was not a typical Christmas in the Hall house. Maybe the quantity of the gifts was mom and dad's way of making up for all of the slim Christmases from years gone by. Maybe they had received a bonus at work or hit it lucky on the lottery and wanted to share the wealth, or they just went overboard that year, who knows. Anyway, that was one Christmas morning I have remembered to this day.

One last note about Christmases at the North Fourth Ave house is that one year I wanted an Electro-Shot Shooting Arcade. I remember asking Santa (mom and dad) for the toy with hopes of getting it. I also remember snooping around the house a bit to see if they had purchased it and hid it somewhere, but no luck there.

Like most Christmases, going to bed early was assured, usually by 8 or 9ish, unless a real good Christmas show was on the television. That particular year on Christmas eve, I woke up in the middle of the night (or what seemed like that time), and as I gathered my senses, I remember hearing the sounds of rat-a-tat-tat, rat-a-tat-tat coming from downstairs. I recognized those sounds from the TV commercials, and I realized then that I was getting my Electro-Shot Shooting Arcade. For you see my dad was right then setting it up and playing with it, or as he would say – testing it out to make sure it worked! I was really excited, but soon I returned to sleep and I'm sure I had a big smile on my face. Happy memories for sure.

Electro-Shot Shooting Gallery by Marx

"We are better throughout the year for having, in spirit, become a child again at Christmastime."
— Laura Ingalls Wilder

Main Street Pet shop – Do Do's Tropical Fish store

Joel Layaw. was a grade school friend of mine. We met when I started attending West Hill Elementary School. Joel lived a few blocks away from me on Rand Street. From time to time, I would walk over to his house, or he'd come to my house and we'd hang out, play some games, etc.

Joel had a lot more hobbies than I had at that time. He was a coin collector, avid major league baseball fan with plenty of sports cards, hockey player and a tropical fish enthusiast. Joel's bedroom had an aquarium in it, and there was also an aquarium in one of the house's downstairs rooms. We spent a lot of time looking at his various collections, especially his coin collection and his aquariums.

There were times when I would walk with Joel to Do Do's Tropical Fish and Pet Supplies store located downtown along Main Street, next door to The Hungry 'I' Restaurant, and down the street west of Powers News. The walk to

the store from Joel's house would take us from Rand Street to First Ave, through the small park like area where we would sometimes play baseball, and then using the set of stairs that

would take us down the hill and across Steele's Creek. This would lead us right onto the western end of Main Street. From there it was a few blocks

Ilion, My Childhood, My Memories

walk heading east, passing Best Garage, National Auto and crossing the
street before the WT Grant store, to the north side of Main Street and ending
at Do Do's pet store. Total walk time was probably fifteen minutes, but a fun
walk when the weather was nice.

**Do Do's Tropical Fish and Pet Supplies. The Main Street building razed
by Urban Renewal in Ilion in the late 1960's.**

Do Do's pet store was not a very large store, but on one of the side walls of
the store it was lined with two-tiered stacked aquariums full of fish, and the
opposite wall had many other pet supplies. In the back of the store, by the
cash register, was usually the store owner standing alongside of a caged area
that housed their pet monkey named Sue (or Susie). From what I have been
told, the monkey was named after the owner's grand-daughter.

The store had that old time – old town look and feel, complete with dark
wooden floors that creaked when you walked on them, large front glass

window, half glass half wood entry door and a high ceiling that I believe may have been a raised tin panel.

Because of the tropical fish, the aquariums needed to be kept in the 76–78-degree range. There were aquarium heaters in each aquarium to regulate the waters temperature, but also the store was kept on the warmer side, which was a real benefit in the winter time, not so much in the summer time. Due to the warmth of the store, and the many aquariums filled with water and fish, the store took on a bit of a humid tropical feel. Throw in the caged monkey and the tropical feel also included a slight hint of urine smell. I would come to know this store and the owners very well over the next couple years as, with Joel's help, I became an actively involved tropical fish enthusiast.

My first aquarium was really a large fish bowl; classic rounded shape with a large circle opening at the top and flat bottom. I believe I started out with some small fish, guppies maybe, but I was soon to learn that there was more than a fish bowl, some fish and food needed to really enjoy this hobby, let alone keep the fish alive for any period of time.

I soon learned of the need for an aquarium air pump, air stone, water filter, water heater, tank thermometer, books on various fish diseases, and the right size aquarium complete with gravel, fish net, plants and other ornaments that provided hiding places for the fish.

Before long I was buying my first real aquarium, a 5-gallon size; a pretty standard size that most people started out with. Adding to that was all the accessories, heater, pump, air-stones, filters, lighted tank cover, gravel, etc. Now this is where the real fun of the hobby soon began.

My parents did not go with me to purchase this complete set up, instead Joel and I walked to the pet shop, purchased the necessary aquarium set-up, and then we carried it all the way back to my house, careful to make sure we took our time avoiding any tripping obstacles that might cause us to drop the glass aquarium. We used the stairs that would take us back up to First Ave and from there we would walk several more blocks to my house on North Fourth Ave, a long distance for sure when carrying the glass aquarium.

The aquarium would be set-up in the den, the same room where we had sanded the floors and found the German coin. The aquarium was put onto a table like stand, one sturdy enough to hold the weight of the aquarium with the water, gravel and all accessories. Total weight would be around 50 pounds as each gallon of water weighed about 8 pounds, then adding in the gravel, the lighted tank lid, and the weight of extra accessories.

Over the next few weeks, I would purchase different fish for the aquarium such as fancy tail guppies (very colorful), swordfish, neon tetras and maybe a bottom feeder such as a cat fish. Once the fish were added I would then sit and watch them for what seemed like hours. They were very interesting to watch as they swam around, interacting with each other, exploring their surroundings, swimming in and out of the castle or shipwreck ornament on the bottom of the tank.

The aquarium needed periodic maintenance as well as adding water to keep the appropriate level. It was my job to take care of all of that, no exceptions. Part of the daily maintenance was to check the temperature, watch the fish for signs of aggression as well as signs of disease, and feed the fish.

The fish food was to be used sparingly as the fish would keep eating as long as food was being added, not healthy for the fish. The fish food not eaten would fall to the gravel where the bottom filter would suck it through the gravel, breaking it down as it passed through. Too much uneaten food would create a buildup of waste and along with the fish waste would mean cleaning the filter more often. It could also lead to altering the pH of the fish water (pH is a measurement of how acidic or alkaline the water is) and that could lead to all kinds of issues including the killing of the fish.

Having the fancy tail guppies added a bit of excitement, as well as added to my learning of where babies come from. The guppies had babies fairly regularly and I would watch and count the babies as they were live birth baby fish. I was soon to learn that I needed to separate the babies from the other fish, as the babies made for a good snack or meal for the more aggressive and bigger fish.

Over the many years since then, I graduated to bigger and more expensive aquarium set-ups, including a few 20-gallon aquariums and a 55-gallon aquarium. Later I would also explore salt water fish, a hobby that needs a lot more daily maintenance, more care than my tropical fish hobby did. The salt water fish were more colorful, more territorial depending on the fish choice, and definitely more expensive, so losing one to negligence of maintenance was costly indeed.

My aquarium hobby lasted into my late thirties and after a few personal house moves, and the resultant loss of some fish due to the moves, not to mention just being busy raising a family, my hobby eventually died out. Though I have often thought of getting back into the hobby, I feel for now I will satisfy my urge by visiting a pet store.

Everyone should have a deep-seated interest or hobby to enrich his mind, add zest to living, and perhaps, depending upon what it is, result in a service to his country. - Dale Carnegie

Ilion, My Childhood, My Memories

Remodeling the house with my Dad and my 'Cast'

Our house on North Fourth Ave went through some major renovations while we lived there. Understand that these renovations were mostly performed by my dad, sometimes with the help of a friend. I remember the chimney in the center of the house being taken down, brick by brick, and the need for the roof to be repaired afterwards. The roof repair was one job that my dad hired extra help for as the roof was pretty steep.

Other renovations included remodeling the only bathroom in the house, which posed an interesting problem when the toilet had to be replaced. The issue was that the plumbing also had to be replaced meaning that it was a much bigger job time wise to complete and there was the issue of eight family members in the house and where would we go to the bathroom in the meantime. Let's just say there was a new use for the current mop bucket and leave it at that.

When it came time to dispose of the clawfoot tub, that was going to be replaced with a new bathtub, my dad thought the best way to get the 2–300-pound tub out of the 2nd floor of the house was through the window of the bathroom. He had taken the window out entirely and with a few friends and some very strong rope, they managed to send the cast iron clawfoot tub out of the second-floor window and onto the ground below. All was well, mostly, for you see that although no person was hurt, the clawfoot tub managed to smash the window on the first floor as it descended to the ground. You know what they say about best laid plans of mice and men, and of course Murphy's law – if anything can go wrong it will.

Besides the chimney and the bathroom, my parents also decided to remodel the kitchen by adding on an addition, and putting in a side entrance to the house that would also facilitate an entrance to the basement. This required a lot of planning, and would involve all of my father's skills from carpentry, to plumbing, to electrical, to insulation, wallboard, shingling, hanging kitchen cabinetry, and much more. This is where I began my working knowledge of those skill sets as I sometimes would hang out with my dad, watching him work, helping where I could and of course being the curious kid that I was, asking many questions.

The spring of my sixth-grade school year I managed to break my thumb. This would be the first of two different times that I broke the thumb on my right hand. This first time it happened is when I had permission during school class to go to the bathroom. Upon entering the bathroom, I noticed a few of my friends, from other classes, also using the facilities.

After completion of the task at hand and then washing our hands, we decided to fool around, pushing each other as kids sometimes do. The pushing then went into play fighting hitting each other in an attempt to claim bathroom dominance – sort of like King of the Hill, only in the bathroom.

Play fighting continued, and got just a bit more physical, and I took a swing, connected and bam – broke my thumb. Now how could a playfight end that way, well you see I did a dumb thing. I tucked my thumb inside of my 4 other fingers making a fist. The way I saw it was that it would give me more striking power, sort of like a hammer head blow. Well, I learned a painful lesson that day, and that is you never, ever tuck your thumb inside of the rest of the fingers when you fight. Cardinal rule number one of fist fighting.

My thumb immediately swelled up, and of course I had to tell the teacher as my thumb was throbbing and painful to the touch. However, what would I tell them about how it happened. I had to quickly make up a story so as not to get my friends and myself in any more trouble.

The story I told was that I had swung open the bathroom door and held my hand out to catch its return only one of the kids called my name and I turned around to see what they wanted and the door swung back onto my thumb.

Ilion, My Childhood, My Memories

The teacher immediately sent me to the principal's office, as we did not have a full-time school nurse for such a small school.

Once I was at the principal's office and explained what had happened, the principal – Mr. Bart Shelley, called my parents and relayed the information to them. When my parents arrived, they chatted briefly with Mr. Shelley and then whisked me off to see Doctor Dennis for an Xray and a cast.

Before I go on, I want to tell you just a bit about principal Bart Shelley. He was a well-known sports official, baseball scout and our principal at West Hill Elementary School. He was a baseball scout for the St. Louis Cardinals and helped Ilion's Charles Frederick "Boots" Day break into the major leagues in 1969 with the St Louis Cardinals. Later 'Boots' Day would play for the Chicago Cubs and the Montreal Expos. Having spent 6 years in the majors and played in 471 games, Day's baseball career found him moving on to coaching positions within the minor leagues.

Bart Shelley was a real good principal, understanding, and hands on. He had a passion for sports and would often be the instructor for after school intermural activity at West Hill School, from kick-ball, to basketball, to dodgeball. He also taught gym when the regular teacher was out sick. The students, including myself, would often say hello to him during the school day and he knew us all by name.

Now, back to my broken thumb. I had a fracture on the thumb below the first knuckle which required a cast to be put on. Doc Dennis didn't put just any cast on, he made sure that the plaster cast wrapped around my thumb, around the palm of my hand, continuing to wrap around my wrist and extended all the way up the arm to my elbow. Today they would probably just put a splint on it, but not in the good 'ole days. Not with Doc Dennis!

The thing about casts is that while the broken bone is healing, you cannot get the cast wet. Not getting it wet meant that you could not clean it, and that would lead to the skin of my arm, inside of the cast, itching. Sometimes it itched so bad that I wanted to rip the cast off my arm in order to scratch it.

Not being able to remove the cast led me to finding other ways to scratch the itch. That meant finding long thin objects that I could squeeze down along the inside of the cast, between the cast and my arm, to try and reach the itching area. Those long thin items could be clothes hangers, mom's cooking spatulas or wooden spoons, a long screwdriver, just about anything that could fit down inside the cast I would use to end the agony of the itch.

The cast needed to stay on for 3 months as compared to today where a splint being used would be on for about 6 weeks. When it came time to take the cast off, it involved the doctor using a small circular bladed saw to cut through the plaster. Let me tell you the first time I saw him with that saw and cutting through my cast, I thought he was going to cut into my arm. Needless to say, he did not, and finally I was free from the cast.

My arm felt strange, lighter and white/gray in appearance, but I could once again scratch to my heart's content. The cast, and my arm both smelled like someone who had not bathed for a while. Thank goodness the cast was off and I was now going home with cast in hand, and a well itched arm.

There's one last thing you need to know about the cast and the adding on of the kitchen addition to our house. While my dad was building the addition to our kitchen, one of the first tasks was to build the floor area and from there you would raise the walls and eventually the roof, thereby completing the outer structure.

When my dad was building the floor, I was helping him. He had the floor joists in place and now he was putting down the plywood subfloor. He used standard plywood and nailed it on top of the floor joists, making the floor. The smell of the plywood as he cut it was a sweet woodsy smell and made a lot of saw dust, which was my job to sweep up.

I enjoyed helping my dad nail the subfloor down, but my cast suffered because of it. You see, I was using my cast like a hammer, hammering the nail into the floor and into the floor joist below. I felt like I had super powers with each nail I pounded in with my cast. However, over time the cast softened and just wore out and soon we were back to the doctors for a cast replacement, and of course a scolding!

After 3 months in the cast, it was great to get it off. It would be a short-lived feeling however, because I was out one day playing baseball in the streets. The batter hit a ball up high into the tree tops that hung over the street, and I was waiting to catch it. Only thing was, I did not have a ball glove on my hand, just my bare hands to catch the ball. When the baseball came down, I was ready – only the ball hit that same thumb, both breaking it and dislocating it, bending the top part of my thumb at the knuckle at almost a 90-degree angle.

While I was straightening my thumb out, I ran into the house to my parents and showed them what had happened. You guessed it, back into the car, back to Doc Dennis, and back into an elbow length cast for the remainder of summer and into the start of my seventh-grade school year. I do not remember if I caught the ball or not, but I like to tell myself that I did!

During construction we still needed to keep the rest of the house clean, as the building dust would find its way into the rest of the rooms. There was the constant sweeping, vacuuming, dusting and washing. Then there were the wood floors in the dining room, living room and den. Besides the sweeping and mopping, those floors needed to be waxed and buffed too.

When the wood floors needed wax and buffing, this would be a time-consuming job, and not an easy one on your knees. I sometimes did that job, as did my older siblings. First you needed to remove the furniture and sweep the floor. Once that was done it was time to mop the floor and wait for it to dry. Then, when it was dry, it was time to apply the Johnson's Paste Wax.

Applying the wax was where it got rough on your knees. For you see you needed to be on your hands and knees on the floor to apply the wax. To apply the wax, you needed a rag and then you would scoop some wax out of the can, as it was a thick paste, then apply it in circular motion in small areas of the floor, and continue this until you have covered the entire floor.

The paste wax would dry to a haze and once it did, it was time for the buffer. We had a Regina duel head floor buffer. This buffer, along with two sets of pads is what we would use to buff out the wax into a nice shiny semi-gloss. The first sets of pads buffed the wax into the floor and again leaving a bit of a haze. Then the second set of pads, more of a shammy type pad would buff the wax into a semi-gloss shine. The floors looked great but it was a lot of work effort to complete.

Side story: I had set up either a race set or perhaps a train set on the floor in the dining room. I was enjoying playing with it when a piece of the track came apart. Trying to reach it, I sort of slid on my knees to the separated track only I took a piece of the wood floor with me. I wound up taking a two-inch size splinter from the wood floor into my knee.

I told my parents about this and that I thought the piece of wood was still in my knee. They looked at my knee, and at the floor area where the piece of wood was taken from, and decided to take me to Doc Dennis to have a look. The doctor probed the area of my knee, feeling around the outside and then taking a stainless-steel probe of sorts, he fished around the opening in my knee where I said the splinter was, and of course he found nothing, only in doing so he was making my knee much sorer; and as with most all wounds, in time it eventually scabbed over.

A couple of weeks had gone by since getting the splinter in my knee, when one morning I woke to go to the bathroom. When I bent my knees to sit down on the toilet, the pressure put upon my knees caused the sliver to come popping out along with a whole lot of puss and liquid. My knee all of a sudden felt like a weight had been lifted, relieved, and the best it had felt in weeks.

The splinter was indeed about two inches long and my parents could not believe the size of it. I am not sure what my parents ever did with the splinter of wood but I was just relieved that it was out. To this day I have a reminder of that time of my life – my youth, that whenever the weather is extremely damp and cold, I have an ache in that knee, like a toothache – dull and a little throbbing.

Part of the house remodeling construction was the foundation that was needed under the addition that we put onto the kitchen. Dad constructed that out of cement blocks and it extended down into the ground at least 4 feet or more. It needed to go that deep to get below the frost line – necessary to prevent heaving from the freeze and thaw of winter.

As the new foundation was placed on the outside of the existing basement it gave mom and dad the idea to have a root cellar there. This required them to insulate it, put plastic on the inside of the insulated walls, plastic on the bottom of the overhead kitchen floor joists, and plastic on top of the rigid insulation laid on the cement floor. They did not heat that space thereby giving them a root cellar for vegetable and fruit storage that would remain a fairly constant and cool temperature from the temperature of the earth below the cement floor and on the outside of the cement block walls.

Mom and dad would often buy bushels of vegetables in the fall time such as squashes, onions and potatoes, typically enough to get us through the winter months. We would also put our apple harvest there too, bushels of the different variety of apples, picked from an orchard, with my favorite being Cortland's.

For you see every fall, sometime around late September, early October, in the wee hours of the morning – 4am-ish as I recall, mom and dad would get up, make coffee, load up the station wagon with empty bushel baskets and prepare to go apple picking! I would either hear them get up, or they would come wake me, as I wanted to go apple picking too. And this particular morning my sister Rosemary had also decided to go with.

Mom got us ready with a thermos filled with coffee for dad, and a thermos filled with hot chocolate for Ro and myself. We then gathered our coats and out the door we went. We drove for what seemed like over an hour to the orchards, and got in line with the other cars, waiting for our turn to enter the orchard.

It was still pretty dark outside when we drove into the orchard and were directed to several trees with the variety of apples that we wanted to pick that morning. I do not remember if dad brought a ladder with or if they had wooden ladders there for us to use, but dad climbed the ladder to get apples that were higher in the tree while Ro and I picked apples from the low hanging branches; or held the flashlight aiming it for dad to see the apples to pick.

We picked bushel after bushel, moving from tree to tree to obtain the varieties we wanted. There were Cortland, Macintosh, Empire, 20 oz and more. And soon, with the morning sun rising, and our bushels now full, it was time to pay up and go home.

I remember on the ride home eating apples, chatting about the picking and wondering just how many apples we had in the several bushel baskets in the back of the station wagon. I also recall one very large apple sitting on the front dash of the car. That apple was the largest I had ever seen and it was the largest we had picked that morning.

That apple, in my young person's mind, was the size of a small pumpkin, about the size of a typical pie pumpkin that you would buy today. I believe dad called it a 20oz apple, a variety of very large sized apples. Apples that are great for cooking with, and especially pie making! I couldn't wait for one of dad's apple pies to be made and having a slice of it warmed with ice cream on the side – ala-mode style!

Side story: My neighbor and friend, Mike Helmer, was visiting me at my house one day. Mom asked us if we'd like a slice of apple pie and if we wanted it ala-mode style. I said yes – please, but Mike said that he would have just the apple pie. Mom prepared the slices of pie and brought it to us. Mike, seeing that mine had ice cream with it, whispered to me that he'd like ice cream too. For you see Mike did not know that Ala-mode meant to add ice cream. Mike and I enjoyed our pie and ice cream! Oh, what fun memories for sure.

Now that we had all of the apples back at the house, dad would carry the bushel baskets down into the root cellar where they would be kept over the next several months. All the while the family would enjoy grabbing an apple from the root cellar and eating it almost any time we wanted. And of course, dad would always make his delicious apple pies!

Side story: Several years later I had found within some of dad's personal papers, a document about his military service indicating that dad had been a cook in the army. I also found out that he was a member of the tank ordinance group and he was stationed at Guadalcanal.

The Guadalcanal Campaign, also known as the Battle of Guadalcanal and codenamed Operation Watchtower by American forces, was a military campaign fought between 7 August 1942 and 9 February 1943 on and around the island of Guadalcanal in the Pacific theater of World War II. It was the first major offensive by Allied forces against the Empire of Japan. — source: Wikipedia

Dad never spoke about the war, but he did come back with his fatigues, his metals, and a souvenir which was the recipe he and the other cooks used for making pie crusts. Mom and dad used that recipe for making all of our holiday pies. However, to first use it they had to revise it, as the original recipe was structured for making dozens of pies at a time and the list of ingrediencies and their respective amounts required for the recipe, needed to be pared down for making perhaps no more than a dozen pies.

I have fond memories of dad making several pies and readying them for the holidays. Pumpkin, cherry, apple and more, and even a minced meat pie! Today my wife uses that same recipe as she does the baking and dessert making, something our kids and grandkids have come to favor very much!

Life is short, eat dessert first! – anonymous

Sunday Dinners at the house

My brother Butch had a very good friend named Alan Hailston. Butch and Alan would hang around a lot at our house, walk downtown and explore the stores and the latest in musical albums. And do things typical teenage boys do in a small town.

They would often attend dances at the high school, or attend a local event at the school. Mostly they went to hit on the girls, or they would go just to pass the time away talking, listening to music and having an occasional cigarette, trying not to get caught while smoking.

Alan is an artist and has done several drawings over the years, mostly pen and ink type drawings. He is also a very good photographer having an eye for color, depth perception, scenery, nature and the like. Alan was also an influence on my brother's photography hobby. My brother's talent was in special effects, lighting, portraits, still life and such. His talents enabled him to win an award for his photograph of a polar bear and her cubs at the Zoo.

Personally, I think the two of them were in a competition to see who could outperform the other with their photography knowledge and talent.

Award winning photo my brother captured of the polar bears at the zoo. Source: Art Hall photo collection

One notable about Alan's artistic capability is that in the gym of the Ilion High School, Alan sketched and then painted the Ilion school logo onto the wall for all to see. When I attended my junior high (7th and 8th grade) at the high school, the logo (pictured) still adorned the gym wall and was displayed there for many years thereafter.

Side story: *The School's Coat of Arms was created by Gary Conover and Dan McGrath IHS Class of 1964. The drawing, by Dan McGrath, is intended to depict Eliphalet Remington. The laurel is for scholarship, and the winged foot represents athletics. Dan and Gary both lettered in track. Source: http://ilionalumni.com/alma.mater.html*

In addition, the Ilion High school had its own school song containing the following lyrics:

The Ilion Alma Mater

*Down among the peaceful valley,
None has such renown,
As our glorious Ilion High School,
And the Gold and Brown.*

*Lift her banner, raise it higher,
Loud her praises sing,
'Till echoing from each hill and valley
Back the answers ring.*

*Still we shout her praises higher,
Sing them loud and strong,
Still we strive to win her glory
All to her renown.*

Lyrics by Edna Brand McGowan, Class of 1905. Edna's words, set to the tune of Cornell's "Far Above Cayuga's Waters", were selected as the winning entry in a contest held to determine the lyrics. (Information provided by Edna's grandson, Richard Parkinson, Class of 1966 and also verified by the Ilion Citizen June 25, 1908 newspaper edition.) source: http://ilionalumni.com/alma.mater.html

Every Sunday mom would cook up a big meal, typically pot roast with all the trimmings, and we would all sit down to dinner usually between 2 and 3pm. Mom did not cook a medium rare pot roast, or any meat medium rare for that matter. Everything she cooked was well done and often required a bit of catsup to help with the swallowing effort.

Mom was a good cook and we never went hungry, its just – well, mom was raised on a farm until she left when she was eighteen. Her mom, my grandmother, would cook up meals for their large family and mom would tell of meals like rabbit, turtle soup, beaver tail soup, and the occasional steak or roast from one of cows that had been taken for slaughter.

Additionally, there were the farm yard chickens that mom would pluck the feathers from after her mom – well, let's just say that her mom helped the chicken on its way to meet its maker. Then the chicken would be prepped, spiced and cooked, and a chicken dinner was enjoyed by all.

I think that perhaps mom saw a bit too much in the way of animal meat preparation and rareness, as well as other unpleasant things on the farm, that from that point on I believe mom cooked all the meat well done, and I'm talking 'Well Done'! (Personally, I like my steak and other meats medium rare.)

Mom would prepare the post roast with the usual potatoes, carrots, celery and onions, and on top of the meat she would apply Lipton's Onion Soup mix. That was pretty much all the seasoning she would add for cooking and any other seasoning such as salt and pepper would be added tableside.

The smell from the cooking would permeate the entire house, and it would make us all hungry. Eating our Sunday meal at 2 or 3 in the afternoon meant we typically were on our own for lunch, meaning that unless we made something for ourselves – or found ready-made snacks, we would not have had much of anything food wise to eat since breakfast. And usually, the only beverages to drink in the house were milk and water, maybe some juice, as it was only on special occasions that mom bought soda-pop with the weekly grocery shopping. This meant that very often you could hear a stomach growl when it was getting close to Sunday dinner time.

For Sunday meals we would always eat in the dining room, not the kitchen. We made sure to set the table with plates, silverware, glasses, napkins, and the appropriate condiments. Most often there was bread or rolls too. This was our Sunday meal time for family to sit together, to chat about the past week, things going on around the neighborhood, or upcoming events.

Pot roast was not always on the Sunday menu, sometimes we would have mom's homemade spaghetti sauce with meatballs and sausage, or we might have meatloaf and mashed potatoes. But most Sundays it was mom's 'Lipton onion soup covered' pot roast with vegetables.

Regardless of the time we ate, at just about 15 minutes before that time there would come a knock at the door. One of us would answer the door, and then the usual sound – 'Butch – Al is here' would ring out. Alan always seemed to know when to show up just before we sat down to eat, like a sixth sense. And this was in the days before any social media, or texting capabilities.

Mom would not refuse anyone a meal, so, very often Alan was invited to join us for Sunday dinner. Funny thing was that Alan never refused a meal either, after all he worked up an appetite walking from his house, up Weisbecker Hill and down our street. Maybe a full mile, regardless of the weather of the day.

Mom would just have us set another place at the table, and pull up another chair.

Alan was always welcomed, given plenty to eat, and then as per the usual schedule, he and Butch would chat afterwards and then Alan was sent on his happy full-stomach way until the next Sunday rolled around.

As for me, I really did not mind Alan being there enjoying the meal with us as I got to listen to Butch and him talk about the goings on at high school and around town. I found the conversation more relaxing and less '21 questions' from our parents asking us about our week.

This became such a common Sunday occurrence that when Alan did not show up, we all began to wonder what had happened to him. He was always welcomed, but at least you'd think that once in a while he might have brought dessert!

Later in life I moved to Rochester NY and found that Alan and his family were living there too. Our families became acquainted with each other, and over the years, we shared many a bar-b-que together, (although I do not remember being invited to many Sunday meals at his house – ha-ha-ha), at least when we did go and visit his family, I got to drink his beer. And of course, a lot of fun was had by all.

During one of the visits, Al and I were reminiscing about Sunday diners and he told me that he would eat lunch around noon at his place and then afterwards he would take a walk and end up at our house to visit with Butch, and he mentioned too that he enjoyed my mom's cooking.

To the memory of those Sunday dinners – **Cheers Al.**

Memories are made when gathered around the dinner table. – anonymous

My many Pets and other creepy things

In my youth I had very few nicknames. Some school taunting names – such as block head, due to the flat shape of the back of my head. Another name they called me was Preacher, due to the dark purple shirt I wore that had a bit of a white color in the front neck area, similar looking to that of a Preacher's shirt. But mostly people just called me Kevin or Kev.

My mom on the other hand had various names for me, such as her favorite name of Fearless Fosdick, after some newspaper comic about a person getting into all types of capers, and having to get himself out of them. But there was one name I dreaded hearing and when mom called me that, I knew for a fact I was going to be in a lot of trouble.

That name was **K E V I N**, usually spoken with an exasperated

yell and with the pronunciation of the name extended for a few seconds longer than it needed to be, and this was a name I had heard often while growing up. As example, I have always been curious about how various items worked and that curiosity has often led me to take the items apart so that I could further study their inner workings. However, in certain instances, when I was not successful in putting the item back together in working order,

and mom found out, it was **K E V I N** what did you do?

Growing up my family we enjoyed having pets in the house, mostly dogs and cats, but I also was fascinated by wildlife in general, and it's here were my

first story involving the use of **K E V I N** begins.

Being inquisitive and somewhat naïve about things, I could be talked into doing things that other kids may have shied away from. For example, picking up a worm, or a frog, or a praying mantis, or a garter snake. One of my friends once convinced me that there were these worms that produce silk and that silk was expensive and you could make some money from raising the worms that produced silk.

I was a trusting person and believed my friend, who then further convinced me that 'Tree Worms', wrap their tree nests in silk that they produce. And all I had to do was to gather a bunch of these tree worms, take them home, put them in water and they would spin a web of silk in order for them to make a home above the water.

At that young age I was excited to make some money, and excited to see how this tree worm experiment would work so I did just that – I gathered tree worms and I put them in a jar to bring home. Once I was home, I followed the instruction I had been given and that was to put the worms into water. So, I filled up the sink in the bathroom in hopes that in the morning, or shortly thereafter I would have some silk.

Later that evening after dinner was done, and after the kitchen was cleaned up, I settled into my bedroom to either do some playing or perhaps some homework. Then as if the Town Cryer of old himself was calling out the time,

I heard that name **KEVIN** – oh crap, what did I do this time?

Rushing through the house to the bathroom, I saw my mom standing there with this look on her face, waiting for an explanation as to what was in her bathroom sink. I told her of how if we left the worms there, we would have silk in the morning. Mom was having none of it and needless to say, my worms were flushed, no silk for me, and to rub salt into the wound – I had to clean up the bathroom squeaky clean.

That would not be the last time for that famous 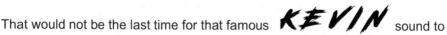 sound to

come from my mom's mouth. Nope, I heard that name used many more times growing up. Though I must admit it gave mom many a story to tell when I was much older and of course, as mothers do, she told the stories in front of my children too.

Our house on North Fourth Ave had two large pine trees in the back yard. These trees towered over the house and eventually they would be taken down before a storm could come and take them down. But until then they were homes to birds and squirrels alike. I would watch the squirrels running around in the trees jumping from branch to branch, chasing each other and just having a fun time. I thought – wouldn't it be nice to have a pet squirrel? This is where my next little story begins.

We would occasionally get some snacks with the groceries, and one of those snacks was peanuts in the shell. One day I decided that maybe the squirrels would like to have some peanuts and just maybe I could train them to take them from my hand.

Gathering up a pocket full of nuts, I went out to the backyard to put my plan into action. I remember standing in between the two trees, peanut in hand, looking into the trees and making a chirping sort of sound to call the squirrels and show them what I had for them. This chirping call to the squirrels went on for a while and my arm was getting tired of holding up the peanut to show the squirrels as I called to them, so I decided to put my arm down to my side.

Looking around the trees, with my hand holding the peanut still at my side, I soon felt a tug on the peanut. I looked down and sure enough there was a squirrel taking the peanut from my hand and just as quick, he scampered away back into the trees. I was excited by this event and I wanted to see if I could do it again and again.

Taking more peanuts from my pocket and making my chirping sounds, it did not take long before again, a squirrel came down to take the peanut. This activity was repeated several more times that day.

Over the next few days and perhaps a couple weeks, I would be able to perform this feat of feeding the squirrels from my hand. There were times that I remember even petting the squirrel between the ears as they took the peanut, cracked it open and ate it right there on the ground besides me. I had successfully trained the squirrel(s) to trust me enough to take the peanuts from my hand.

One day while I was inside playing, I heard that infamous name again being called by my mom — **KEVIN** — uh-oh what had I done now...

Running to the kitchen there stood my mom, with that look on her face, again, pointing to the sliding glass door we had installed in the kitchen addition that overlooked the backyard. On the other side of the glass door was not one, not two, not even three, but five squirrels standing on their hind legs, leaning against the door and looking into the house.

Needless to say, my squirrel feeding days ended right then, and moms' words of **'GET RID OF THEM'** echoed in my head for a few days more. Mom did not like squirrels and often referred to them as rats with fluffy tails. With the squirrels no longer receiving food from me they retreated back into the trees.

Of course, we had other pets that we did keep in the house, besides my fish aquarium. We had a dog named Pep, a mutt of many breeds, and occasionally a cat, and then there was the pet rabbit. For the most part we treated the pets like any member of the family. They went outside and played with us, laid on the floor with us, or joined us in the chair as we sat and watched TV.

The most interesting of these pets was the rabbit. This was the first unusual family pet we had, but again we treated it like one of the family. We fed it by placing a dish alongside the dog's dish. We bathed it and we had a litter box for it to do its business.

We would often sit in the easy chair and hold the rabbit and pet it while we watched TV. That is until the rabbit initiated each one of us, one by one as we sat in the chair petting it. I think the rabbit was a bit confused about where to go to the bathroom. By the way – I was the last to be initiated. You know what they say about saving the BEST for last!

When we moved to Minnesota, my parents gave the rabbit to one of their friends who owned a farm, and that was the last rabbit pet we ever had.

Today I live in a rural area with land that backs to a forever wild section of town with plenty of trees, and wildlife to enjoy. I keep teasing my wife about having pet squirrels or pet deer (that seem to inundate our yard and constantly rob the bird feeders). Like my mom, my wife has made it clear that she is having none of that – so I'm destined to not live my life dream of having pets like that. That is unless I want to forever hear that name being called…

K E V I N!!!

On Top of Old Baldy all covered with Students

Behind the Ilion High School is the back side of Armory Cemetery, and adjacent to that is a hill that has been nicknamed Old Baldy. This hill borders the access roadway in back of the school and is across from the school building and the football field.

If you were to walk to the top of the hill and continue walking, you would end up entering the southwest side of Russell Park. A park I visited as a youth growing up in Ilion. A park for picnicking in the summer and sledding in the winter. A park that had swings and a merry go round that I can remember just spinning around on, round and round and round until I was almost sick. And I remember the wintertime and the old toboggan we had
that seated six of us kids. I can also remember my dad taking us all in the station wagon to the Russell Park 'Bowl', a big and deep cut-out area within the hilly landside that made for a fabulous sledding hill.

Dressed in your coat, hats, mittens (that often got soaking wet over the day's activity), and those winter rubber boots. The boots that buckled up the front, that before putting them on, you would take old bread wrappers – the kind that bread came in, the kind with the logo of the company that produced it, displayed for all to see,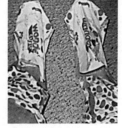
many of them having the 'Wonder' logo on them – placing each foot into an individual wrapper before putting on the boot. Doing this would enable your feet to stay dryer longer as you enjoyed your day of tobogganing and sledding in Russell Park.

On a given weekend, providing there was enough snow, you could find perhaps a hundred or more kids and parents sledding down that hill. The ride down for a child was exhilarating, but the walk back up the hill was a chore, especially pulling the sled or toboggan behind you. This was both a fun time and a tiring time.

However, it was Old Baldy that was most famous amongst the high school students. It has been the backdrop for many Yearbook pictures over the years. It has been a seating place to watch the sporting events happening on the football field, and it has been a resting place to sit and talk with a friend. But mostly it is famous or infamous, as the students would say, for the gym teachers and sports coaches making the student run 'wind sprints' up the hill repeatedly to the point of almost puking. As the coaches would say, it toughens you up – builds character...I think however, many a student/player would find exception in that statement.

lion High School graduating class of 1969 sitting on 'Old Baldy', source: 1969 Ilion Mirror Yearbook

This hill could be especially nasty when it got wet and slippery. And this hill could be your nemesis when you acted up a bit in gym class and the teacher was feeling especially irritated. This hill could also be a fun time for playing King of the Hill. A game that sometimes the students would play after class or during lunch hour. This is where my Old-Baldy hill experience begins.

I was around 12/13 years old at the time and now attending classes at the high school. At that time the 7th and 8th grade students were separated from the 9th – 12th grade students, by having their own wing of the high school where they would attend class. The Gym, Library and the Cafeteria were shared resources for the full high school; however, the cafeteria schedules were adjusted to keep the students separated, and the gym had a partition down the center which was often deployed in order to keep these students' classes separated.

Back then, I would walk at least a mile and a half if not a bit more to school one way, regardless of the weather. To ride a bus at that time, you needed to be more than two miles from the school. My mom and dad both worked, but before they left for work, they would always remind us to go straight home after school. This message sometimes fell on deaf ears for me as I would want to hang out a bit and chat with friends, or even explore Ilion a bit more and take other routes home. Routes that were not always the straight ones.

One day after school, a group of kids were playing 'King of the Hill' on Old Baldy. I wanted to play along with them even though my parent's message was ringing in my ear to come straight home. I decided to stay and play anyways.

We had fun that afternoon running up the hill, trying to take over the top of it from the group of kids that had claimed it. We would launch different offenses, sometimes our full group rushing up the hill at the same time, sometimes splitting the group into two or more groups and launching an attack on several fronts.

We made several attempts that afternoon and had reached the top or near the top when we would be caught or repelled and sent back down the hill to regroup and try a new strategy. On one such attempt I remember running up the hill, but I ran into the opposition. Turning to dodge the capture I slipped and went down on my side, shoulder first, sliding down the hill for a few feet.

I was winded a bit from the fall, but managed to get back up, feeling some discomfort and slight pain in my shoulder. I brushed it off figuring I had probably bruised my shoulder when I hit the ground. But I was later to find out I had done more damage than that.

My shoulder ached a bit over the next few days, and I began to notice a swelling, a lump of sorts in my armpit. I was a bit worried as to what it might have been, but I was more worried what my parents would do if they knew I did not come straight home, that I had stopped to play on Old Baldy and during that time I had caused an injury to myself.

The fear of the physical pain versus the fear of emotional pain was causing an internal conflict for sure. I eventually decided to ride it out with hopes that my arm would heal and no one would be the wiser.

It took several weeks for the lump to go down, but it did not disappear entirely. To this day if I have been working out or doing physical work around the house, I can still feel a bit of a lump in that arm pit. Never the less, that injury has not slowed me down and has not prevented me from doing things of a physical nature.

Many years later, having totally forgotten about the incident on that hill, I went in for my yearly doctor visit and physical. Actually, given that I have a strong dislike for doctor offices, it was probably a five-year doctor visit and physical.

The doctor did the typical routine, starting with asking a bunch of questions, some which really had nothing to do with my health, but was questions he was forced by law to ask. I'll save those questions for another time perhaps. The doctor also would take my temperature, weight, blood pressure, look in my throat and ears, and of course check me for a hernia and prostate – an uncomfortable exam and one that many late night and stand-up comedians have made fun about for years. He then would have me stand straight to check my spine, and have me bend over to touch my toes, all to check for signs of scoliosis. It was during this test that he noticed something.

When the test was over, we reviewed what he had found and talked over the suggestions he had for continued maintenance and health improvement. Mostly I was healthy but there were a couple of things he wanted to advise me on. First was my blood pressure. It was a bit high, but as he noted that this was not the first time that I had high BP in his office, and that it most likely had something to do with 'White Coat Syndrome', but it was also more than that as I was already on medication for the blood pressure.

After that discussion he then asked me about my shoulder. He asked if I had ever injured it. Thinking back on it I began to recall the time on Old Baldy and I related the story to the doctor. He then asked to see my arm pit area, for which he also felt around a bit, it kind of tickled.

He concluded the exam by telling me that at the time of the fall on Old Baldy I probably had dislocated my shoulder and maybe even tore some ligaments. He reached that conclusion because he noticed that as I stood straight that one of my shoulders was lower than the other. And after he had examined both my shoulder and armpit area, that he was certain that I had sustained an injury, and that most likely it had happened during that fall.

I remember him advising me that there was nothing to be done now, but that I might get more aches and pains in that shoulder as I aged. He also advised that there was a good chance for some arthritis to make an appearance as time went by. But for now, things are good. I can still play with my grandchildren, and no real pain as of yet. I do however wonder what would have happened had I told my parents when the injury occurred on Old Baldy and we had paid a visit to good 'ole Doc Dennis at that time.

We can never know what might have been but what is to come is another matter entirely - C. S. Lewis

A view looking east at Ilion High School and the newly completed Weber Ave. Elementary School (later the junior high wing) with "Old Baldy" at the top center c.1960

View looking northeast at Ilion High School and the Weber Ave. Elementary (later the junior high wing) with snow covered "Old Baldy" at the right of the photo in 1961.

View looking Northeast of Old Baldy on the right and the back side of Ilion High School in the background

Ilion Central School's nickname of the "Golden Bomber" can be traced back to the year 1935. A reporter from the Utica OBSERVER-DISPATCH by the name of William Malloy used the reference in his write-ups of the 1935 football squad. In that year, the Ilion team was outfitted in beautiful gold uniforms. The name seemed to stick, and since that time has become the nickname associated with the school in all of their activities. Joe Bemis provided this bit of Ilion history to Ilion's Principal in 1977 and it was reported in the Utica Observer Dispatch. – 10/27/1977

Ilion, the Town Remington Arms Built and Urban Renewal Destroyed

This chapter discusses the effects of Urban Renewal and its implementation of the 'Master Plan', on the village of Ilion and its residents. I wanted to address here that I am of the belief that Urban Renewal did indeed negatively impact the village of Ilion. That it reduced the number of businesses, thereby reducing the need for laborers and ultimately leading residents to seek employment elsewhere and in many cases leave Ilion and New York State.

My viewpoint is that the remnants of today's Ilion offer little in the way of a community that was once rich in history and culture. A village that once:

- made history by the building of products that were utilized around the world and in doing so employed thousands.
- offered its residents and other nearby towns shoppers everything from apples, to clothing, to toys, to tires and zucchini.
- was walked around in by parent and children alike.
- honored its culture and traditions and respected its residents.
- made residents proud to say: We're from Ilion and no-one could be prouder! Proud of the *Gold and Brown!*

I long for the Ilion of old, the memories that it held for me, the friends, the stores and their owners, and the feeling of belonging. If you are not of this line of thought, and believe that Urban Renewal was a good thing for the town of Ilion and its residents, then you may want to skip the rest of this chapter.

Change for change sake, is a recipe for failure.
Dr. Travis J. Hendrick

Ilion, My Childhood, My Memories

I believe that no book that is associated with Ilion NY could be or should be written without the mentioning of the Remington's and the firearms' company that they built within the town. How over the years that company gave employment to the townspeople and the surrounding communities and ultimately helped to shape the town into the Ilion I knew as a kid, a type of town not unlike the television show *The Andy Griffith Show*, and that show's town of Mayberry. That is until 'Urban Renewal' (UR) happened and dramatically changed the face of the town...but let's start my story nearer the beginning.

The Remington Company was founded in 1816 as Eliphalet Remington II (1793–1861) believed he could build a better gun than he could buy. Remington began designing and building a flintlock rifle for himself. At the age of 23 (in late 1816), he entered a shooting match and although he finished second, his well-made gun impressed many of the other contestants. Before Remington left the field that day, he had received so many orders from other competitors that he had officially entered the gunsmithing business. By 1828, he moved his operation to nearby Ilion, and it is this site that is still used by the modern Remington firearms plant.

After the Civil War, the Remington arms company went through some tough economic times and on March 7, 1888, ownership of E. Remington & Sons was auctioned by court order and the highest bidder was new owners, Marcellus Hartley and Partners – **see *Appendix 3 The Auction of Remington Arms*.** This partnership consisted of Hartley and Graham of New York, New York, a major sporting goods chain who also owned the Union Metallic Cartridge Company in Bridgeport, and the Winchester Repeating Arms Company of New Haven, both in Connecticut. At this time the name was formally changed to the Remington Arms Company. The Bridgeport site became the home of Remington's ammunition plant.

Remington has been a staple in Ilion since 1828, providing employment to tens of thousands of employees over the decades. Ilion was a town built upon this employment, and Remington, as the main employer, would provide many families living wages and benefits; affording them the ability to build homes throughout Ilion and the Mohawk Valley.

Remington Arms and its museum – Hoefler Ave looking west

Several of my relatives have worked at Remington over the years; my grandpa, uncles and cousins. My mom, my brother Butch and I also worked at Remington during the late 1970's and early 1980's. My job there was classified as a 'floater'; where I would operate various machines, making eyepieces, breech rings and barrel site ramps to name a few.

Working at Remington afforded my wife and I to buy our first home on Marshall Ave in Ilion, afforded us a new car, and enabled me to attend Herkimer County Community College, where I would receive an A.A.S. degree in Computer Science.

During my last semester of college, my family grew with the birth of my son Kristofer. Upon graduation in 1981, I started my computer programming career at Eastman Kodak Company, moving my family to Rochester NY, and growing our family with the birth of our daughter Jennifer. And the rest as they say is history! That history, the Rochester part of my life will have to wait for another time to discuss.

Remington, town businesses and other growing businesses, such as nearby Mohawk Data Science – who developed the first Key to Tape machine, helped to grow both the economy and Ilion residency, reaching an all-time high of 10,199 people in the 1960 census. However, since then the decline in population has been on-going, resulting in the 2020 population census of 7,646 residents, and a drop of over 2,500 people – one quarter of the population of 1960.

You might ask why this happened and how could a bustling town like Ilion was at the time, lose so many people over the course of a few decades. I don't have all the answers, but I think part of the reason was the Urban Renewal programs with the destruction/construction activities undertaken in downtown Ilion, that were guided (or mis-guided) by the '***Master Plan***'.

In the book titled <u>Worked Over</u> by Dimitra Doukas, Ms. Doukas described the Master Plan as follows:

> ***The Mater Plan: Village of Ilion, NY*** *laid out the "programs necessary for the Village to remain a modern progressive village". The plan was to "rejuvenate" what the planners called the central business district by replacing the "blighted" and "obsolete structures" with "sound, tax producing property".*

She further goes on to state that this so called "blight" was hard to find in Ilion's tidy downtown.

> *Urban renewal proponents took thousands of photos (now in the Ilion Library Historical Room collection), but to get shots of "blighted and obsolete" structures they had to step into the back alleys where they could achieve a certain **West Side Story** look with shots of fire escapes, garbage cans, and laundry hanging out to dry from second-story apartments.*

And further as she reported in her book:

> *A Vietnam veteran "wept" he told me, when they demolished the landmarks of his childhood. "They" were telling everybody that the buildings were not "structurally sound", but that he said was a lie. He and his sister watched, and counted. The wrecking ball hit one building twenty-seven times before it "even dented that old brick".*
>
> *"It breaks my heart", a library patron told me. "They took away a part of my life I'll never get back".*

In the end, Ilion downtown went through a major renovation starting in 1967 and was completed for the most part in 1973. Essentially all of the downtown stores along Mainstreet west of Otsego to First Street and including Union Street were razed. And in some ways, it does bother me to say that my uncle, Don Hall, was the Executive Director overseeing the project.

As a result of Ilion's Urban Renewal, Ilion's historic Main Street, with its renowned building blocks such as Powers/Thompson, Union, and Hotaling, were all gone, and in its place was a small pedestrian shopping plaza called the Keystop Mall (about the size of a super Walmart) had become the new face of the village. Later it would be called by the name of Fay's Mall.

Fays Drug was the anchor store to the multi-store (approx. 9 additional stores) mall. Fays was more than a drug store, also selling shoes, clothes, toys, and the like. Initially the mall stores employed many towns people including my wife, Sharon. Overtime however the mall and the town lost its luster and began losing population. Several years later Fays Mall would turn into a medical center complete with lab and doctor offices.

The destruction of the downtown area in the name of progress, in my opinion, was anything but progress. Sold to the townspeople as necessary because of **'the blight existing within the buildings of the business district'**. If it was that much of a blight, why not also take down the Remington buildings too, as some of them were older than the buildings UR destroyed. For me this may have been nothing more than a way to spend available federal government money, while maybe filling some pockets of those involved too. Perhaps, this blight was nothing more than **'dubiously staged photos'** with gray overcast skies as the backdrop, as Dimitra Doukas has pointed out in her book.

I would argue that the same urban renewal money could have been more wisely spent updating the current buildings that the many downtown businesses had occupied. And I further argue that the ending cost would have been less than the total spent on the Urban Renewal program, and the once vibrant town, having been renovated could be returned to the residents with a facelift, leaving both memory and its history intact.

This of course is conjecture on my part, but before you agree or disagree, let me tell you more of my childhood in Ilion, and the downtown I knew and walked safely as a child from 6/7 years of age until I moved when I was 14. Let me tell you about the stores, the Capitol movie theater, the Christmas events and the Fire Station with the arrival of Santa Claus via a helicopter.

Let me tell you of the town where I rode my bike with my friends to the little league baseball field as part of the Ilion Tigers Little League team. And let me tell you about a town that I grew up in and where time almost stopped while the radiance of the residents shown bright. A town that watched out for everyone, but perhaps failed when it was needed most. Let me tell you of my home town of Ilion.

"I don't think I've changed all that much from a kid who grew up in a small town". – Alan Jackson

Mainstreet stretched for what seemed like miles to me as a child. I could walk north from my house at the time, along Central Ave to Mainstreet. I could walk east down Mainstreet past Remington Arms plant, which was surrounded by an iron fence that ran along the sidewalk by the street.

I would usually carry a stick with me so that I could drag it along the Remington Arms fence, making a rat-a-tat-tat sound similar to that of putting a baseball card on the tire spokes of your bicycle. Later, during the urban renewal that portion of Mainstreet was sold off to Remington Arms and a new iron fence was put across the roadway blocking off the road and sidewalk to all pedestrians.

Crossing the street, I would walk along the north side and head back west towards the center of town. Continuing down Mainstreet past the intersection of Otsego Street and across to the block that contains many stores such as Powers News, The Hungry 'I' restaurant and Do Do's Pet Store.

Remington Arms – Main Street looking East, showing the iron fence by the sidewalk that I would run my stick against. Source: Joe Smith collection

Entering the front of Powers News you would often see many towns people chatting, drinking coffee, buying the newspaper and the like. You could continue through the store and exit out the back door into an alleyway that ran between the block of stores and the Fire Station.

The Fire Station was the place where I would go at Christmas time as they would always have Santa Claus arrive there, greet the children and hand out candy. This was not just an ordinary Santa Claus meet and greet, Santa was flown into the fire station arriving via helicopter flown by Francis 'Bill' DeJohn (a town resident). This was a site most engaging, widening the eyes of children and adults alike. This event was a yearly tradition. Though not one that I was fortunate enough to attend every year.

The above and below pictures shows the back of Mainstreet shops and the Ilion Fire Station.

Ilion, My Childhood, My Memories

Urban renewal removed all the shops from the fire station South to First Street. Done in the name of progress – according to the Mater Plan to 'remain a modern progressive village', but turned out in the long run to further 'deteriorate' the town of Ilion, at least that is my opinion.

Gone were the overhead power lines and phone wires along MainStreet where the Christmas lighted garland decorations were hung. Gone were the shops with the various holiday displays. Gone were the shop owner personalities that made the shopping experience more meaningful. Gone were the town smells and noises that let you know you were in your hometown community.

Gone were the National Auto Store, The Best Garage, WT Grant, Powers News, Do Do's Tropical Fish Store, The Hungry 'I' restaurant, Bonns, Dentist offices, Freemans Store, J. Panaritas restaurant, the Capitol movie theater, The Oddfellow Temple, Jays, and many other places of interest. Gone were the store owners who gave life to downtown, who opened their store doors every day to town residents.

Gone were the store shoppers walking the street and, who as they shopped, saying hello to passerby's, often stopping to chat with those whom they knew to get caught up on the current news of the day or the latest family updates. Gone were decades upon decades of local history, torn down and taken away to be buried in a landfill somewhere. Gone was the heart of the town – gone was the life blood of the town called Ilion.

Gone But Not Forgotten

Replaced by a cold gray cement box-like building that was out of place in a historic town. Replaced by an uninviting humdrum walking environment lacking of any real ambience. Replaced by material that had not known the historic timeline of the town and the character of buildings it had replaced. Constructed with a new main road that drove you around the town instead of

Ilion, My Childhood, My Memories

through the downtown. Tearing out the original and strong beating heart of the old town, and replaced by a sleek new artificial heart that would not be able to stand the test of time, done, as the Master Plan said, to 'remain a modern progressive village'.

The question of Urban Renewal being good for the longevity of Ilion, and future generations of Ilionites is still a debated (both factually and emotionally) question today. I can say that from research I have done on the subject, and from my own experience of growing up in Ilion, and adding in governmental Census data of both population, unemployment and poverty of Ilion; that in my opinion Urban Renewal did not accomplish the goals that the Ilion governments of the time, and UR planners of the time had promised.

As pointed out in Joe Collea's latest book: _Our Town: Ilion, New York – A selective look at 300 years of history_; on pages 316 Joe has stated that:

> "To those too young to have experienced a walk downtown a half-century ago through the small but welcoming web of streets, yes you did miss something special. In its pre-urban renewal days, Ilion was a quaint, old village…but mindfully one that was aging more with each succeeding year. Just like many of us who still mourn its passing, the countenance of the Ilion, circa 1959 and sans the intervening urban renewal, would not have looked the same today anyway. The aging process can be just as devastating and disfiguring on structures of brick and mortar as it is on bodies of flesh and bone."

In Dimitra Doukas's book: _Worked Over- The Corporate Sabotage of an American Community_, she has researched that in 1952 the Ilion City Directory had listed 270 businesses and by 1970 with the loss of the Rand Corp., Univac and with Urban Renewal plans for demolition, Ilion had just 199 businesses. And after Urban Renewal completion and by 1994 only 112 businesses remained in the village. As she states on page 141 of her book;

"The village lost close to half of its business establishments since the 'rejuvenation' of the central business district. Urban Renewal was decidedly not good for business."

I have done my own research to decide if UR had a good or bad impact on Ilion and Ilionites. I have looked at data from many years and many sources in order to create these charts as accurately as the data allowed. The following highlight that research and I offer this for your own decision making.

Historical population [1]		
Census	Pop.	%±
1870	2,876	—
1880	3,711	29.00%
1890	4,057	9.30%
1900	5,138	26.60%
1910	6,588	28.20%
1920	10,169	54.40%
1930	9,890	-2.7%
1940	8,927	-9.7%
1950	9,363	4.90%
1960	10,199	8.90%
1970	9,808	-3.8%
1980	9,450	-3.7%
1990	8,888	-5.9%
2000	8,610	-3.1%
2010	8,053	-6.5%
2020 [2]	7,646	-5.1%

Urban Renewal Timeframe '67 – '73

Source:
1. "Census of Population and Housing". Census.gov. Retrieved June 4, 2015
2. U.S. Census Bureau QuickFacts: Ilion village, New York

The graph to the left shows the population from 1870 through 2020. I have indicated the years of Urban Renewal (UR) and note the after population decline of Ilion NY. The fact that population has declined steadily after UR can be attributed to multiple factors:

- UR had reduced businesses in Ilion from 199 (1970) – 112 (1994)
- NY State decline of population from 1970 through today
- Lack of available jobs in the valley
- Political climate of state government not business friendly
- Political Anti-gun pressure being brought to bear upon Remington Arms
- Parents/Grandparents moving to where children/grandchildren are located
- Decline in number of births/family and aging population deaths

Overall, however, you do have to question the obvious decline in Ilion's population after Urban Renewal completion. And ask yourself – was UR really successful for Ilion and its residents, or perhaps only successful for

Ilion, My Childhood, My Memories

those intimately associated with the Master Plan (and the implementation of its goals), and those few astute business minded people who stood to benefit from the destruction of Ilion's downtown?

The chart to the right shows the Unemployment and Poverty percentages of Ilion from 1970 – 2022, (as a percentage of its population). It is clear from this chart and the previous one for Population, that they depict the overall declining environment in Ilion NY. One can argue, therefore that UR was bad for Ilion's overall survival. One can also argue that there are more circumstances that have led to the decline of Ilion's environment over this 52 year period that are beyond UR's effect.

Statistical Data Analysis	2022 Ilion, NY	2022 NY State	2022 Natl Avg	1970 Ilion NY	1970 NY state	1970 Natl Avg.
Unemployment	8.30%	6.2%[7]	4%	7.5%[3]	4.4%[1]	4.50%
Poverty [2]						13%
		12.7%				10.4%[6]
	20.9%	13.9%[8]	12.30%	10.4%[5]	8%[4]	13.7%[9]

1. Jobless Rate Ebbing, State Statistics Show - The New York Times (nytimes.com).
2. 50 years of US Poverty: 1960 – 2010, Newgeography.com – this link contains real good information about rates of poverty over 50 year period.
3. Herkimer Evening Telegram 8/9/1971 - State's Economy Steady
4. Adirondack Almanack 6/4/2019: 40 years of Poverty in Rural America www.adirondackalmanack.com/2019/40-years-of-poverty-rate-trends-in-rural-America.html
5. IBID – Rural NY Towns Table 6
6. IBID
7. Fred Economic Research 1/26/2022 Unemployment Rate in NY table – sourced US Bureau of Labor Statistics HTTPS://Fred.Stlouis.org/series/NYUR
8. Chart: Poverty Rate By State 2022 HTTPS://worldpopulationreview.com/state-rankings/poverty-rate-by-state
9. US Poverty and Income Inequality Rise from 1970 levels: Study HTTPS://IBtimes.co.uk/us-poverty-income-inequality-rise-1970-levels-study-1453890

Joe Collea in his book: ___Our Town: Ilion, New York a selective look at 300 years of history,___ continuing on with page 316, states:

> "Unfortunately, nostalgia often has a way of clouding rational judgement. Was life in Ilion back in the day better than life today? How much of that perceived satisfaction was the result of the existence of a few streets and several rows of buildings? A little, some or a lot? The answer depends upon your individual perspective as much as anything"

Side note: Joe Collea was my 7th and 8th grade history teacher at Ilion High School (Junior High). And as I have recently discussed with him, though he tried hard to make his classroom teaching interesting and to keep my and others attention, at that time I was not really fond of history. As I have aged, gaining both experience and wisdom (hopefully), I find that history is just as important to learn from as is today's news items. Having a new found respect for what the U.S.'s and world history was and how we have arrived at this point in time, better grounds me in my understanding of current events.

History is important. More than any other topic, it is about us. Whether one deems our present society wonderous or awful or both, history reveals how we got to this point. – James W. Loewen

The town that Remington Arms help build, the town the residents grew into a community, the town that gave back much to its residents, and the rest of the world for that matter, now forever changed. In this authors opinion, it was destroyed by the 'Master Plan' – in order 'to remain a modern progressive village', and the legacy of what was called Urban Renewal.

We may never know the final answer of UR being good or bad for Ilion and Ilionites. But one thing is for sure, Ilion's decline is ongoing and unless new business is brought into the greater Mohawk Valley, it just might be a matter of time before Ilion and other towns within the Mohawk Valley decide to merge into one, as has been the case for some of their local school systems.

I moved from Ilion in the summer of 1971 as my dad was transferred with his job to Minnesota. And I would temporarily move back in 1976, with my wife, to begin the next chapter of my life. A life that would see me graduate from college, move to Rochester, NY (1981) for the start of my career and to raise a family. A life filled with adventure as well as challenges. A life enhanced by memories of my childhood and the town I grew up in. Memories of a town long since gone, and a simpler time of my life, still resonating with me as I watch my own grandchildren grow up in this fast paced and sometimes confusing world, we are now living in.

I would learn that the term given to this feeling is **Hiraeth**. Hiraeth is a Welsh word for longing or nostalgia, an earnest longing or desire, or a sense of regret. The feeling of longing for a home that no longer exists. A deep and irrational bond felt with a time, era, place or person. Such is my feeling of, and longing for, the old-childhood town I grew up in, my home town called Ilion.

Sometimes you never know the value of a moment until it becomes a memory.
Dr. Seuss

Ilion has offered much to its residents, to NY State, to the United States and to the world (**see Appendix 4, Firsts for Ilion, NY**). I am hopeful that the village of Ilion will renew itself, and once again become a vibrant and successful community. That it will rise like the Phoenix of lore and become an active and vibrant community for future generations of beloved Ilionites, and for their bike riding, baseball playing, tobogganing, swimming, snowball throwing and friendship loving children!

Hope rises like a phoenix from the ashes of shattered dreams. – S. A. Sachs

Personal Reflection

When I was writing this book, I reflected upon the many stories and photos I wanted to include. Stories that I had recalled from my youth, many of them with vivid detail. Certain stories did not make it into the book, such as stories of dirt clump fights with friends, my first fist fight with a person of dislike, my first kiss by a girl in second grade, and even my first real girl crush in eighth grade. Stories that have special memories for me, but ones I'll keep to share at a later time perhaps.

Many of the stories I reviewed for this book made me smile, made me feel a comfort and calm peaceful feeling; while others made me laugh out loud remembering the fun and perhaps craziness of the occasion. And still others reminded me of life events and the messages from those events, and the life lessons that were presented.

And then there are the many photos, such as those of my family members and friends that had passed away, and the many 'before' and 'after' pictures of my boyhood town of Ilion, again very meaningful to me. For those photos that were selected to be included, they were done so with special care to help illustrate the story line. Those not selected, still special in their memory, but will remain for now within their own picture albums or respective website links.

I must admit that at times I felt a wash of different emotions, beyond those of joy and wonderment, come over me as I processed the stories and especially the photos; not unlike the emotions you might feel when a loved one passes away. I found that I had gone through what is typically described as the Five Stages of dealing with death: Denial, Anger, Bargaining, Depression and Acceptance. Only for me it was more like going on a long drive through a roadway of emotions with many stops at such places of: sadness, denial, anger, anxiousness, frustration, sympathy and solitude. Each stop along that road allowing me to further process the emotion felt by what the story and/or photo had meant. And now, with the final words of my story having written, I am finally nearing acceptance, and a 'freedom' or 'release' of sorts like a catharsis of those many emotions.

I have come to the conclusion that I must accept that the past is the past, and that I cannot change that. I must now take comfort in knowing that for a brief period, I had the pleasure of living in and enjoying one of the best hometowns imaginable. A place of many wonders, of much history and tradition, and a place where I made some fabulous childhood memories. I must accept that the Ilion of my youth can now only exist in photographs and in my memory. And I know too, that I can keep it alive through my storytelling.

For now, 'Old Ilion' is a time capsule full of your own memories, and available for you to unlock, to open up and to enjoy when the occasion arises. – Kevin M Hall

I now leave you with this 'trinket' that for posterity is a story presented in written format – a bunch of white paper with black marks on them which for the reader have chronicled my boyhood experiences. And as for me – my time growing up in Ilion is forever cherished within my heart and its beauty is forever kept alive within my memories.

Life goes on…whether you choose to move on and take a chance in the unknown, or stay behind, locked in the past, thinking of what could've been. – unknown

Ilion, My Childhood, My Memories

Ilion – a look to the past

The following several pages highlight some of the buildings and stores that made Ilion a unique town to grow up in. Many of the pictures included in the following pages, unless otherwise noted, came from sources such as the **Ilion Free Public Library Historical Room**, Facebook groups **"Ilion Rembers" and "Ilion Remembers"**, newspapers: **The Ilion Sentinel and the Evening Telegram,** Internet search results, **Http://Ilion.faithweb.com/photo.html (the Joe Smith collection which contains a large collection of pictures of old Ilion)**, the 1968 Ilion Mirror Yearbook, and the **authors personal photo collection**.

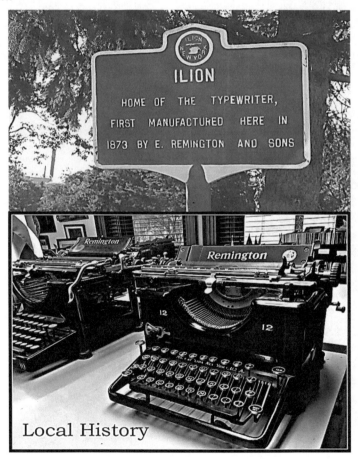

Ilion, My Childhood, My Memories

Noon Day Bustle

Main Street, looking West, Ilion, N.Y.

217596

Ilion, My Childhood, My Memories
106

Ilion, New York

Post Card From Rick Englebrecht's Collection-Scanned By Ginny Miller In 2005

Capitol Theatre, Ilion, N. Y.

The Capitol Theater, located on Otsego Street looking South

Ilion, My Childhood, My Memories

107

Methodist Church on Second Street, Ilion NY

In April 1864, steps were taken to build the Methodist Church. It was planned to build it of cut stone, similar to that in the first story, but the stone further down in the quarry was found to be too soft, so the Church was completed in red brick.

In 1890 the Remington Memorial Chapel was added to the Church. It was given by Caroline A. Remington in memory of her husband, Philo Remington. This church has had a useful and vigorous life for over 150 years. We feel confident that, with God's guidance and the active cooperation of the membership, this Church will continue its life for many years to come.

This was my church, my Sunday school classroom, and provided the instruction and teachings necessary in creating my religious foundation.

ODD FELLOWS TEMPLE AND TEMPLE THEATRE.
ILION N Y

Odd Fellow Temple torn down as part of Urban renewal in the late 1960's.

As part of the urban renewal efforts of late 1960's most of Otsego Street business from the Capitol movie theater looking north to Main Street were all razed, including the buildings viewed at the North end of Otsego on Main Street.

The Bouncing Bear as found in the 1968 Ilion Mirror Yearbook (source), originally drawn by Alan Hailston (class of 1970).

If History were taught in the form of stories, it would never be forgotten! – Rudyard Kipling

Centennial Whisker Contest At The Capital Theatre In Ilion, NY 1952

**Inside the Capitol movie theater, for the Centennial Whisker Contest.
Note the Balcony, and the details on the ceiling.**

The front buildings, bordering old Main Street and Central Ave, contained Powers News, the Hungry 'I' restaurant, Lawyer and Dental offices, and Do Do's Pet shop amongst other businesses (Pre-Urban Renewal). Behind it is the Ilion Fire Station. The fire station still exists but the street of shops was razed during the urban renewal project in the late 1960's.

Corner of old Main Street and Otsego Street looking west Pre-Urban Renewal

Corner of old Central Ave and Main Street looking west Pre-Urban Renewal. You can see some of the old brick that one time lined the street poking through the pavement.

Ilion, My Childhood, My Memories

113

Main Street looking East, Pre-Urban Renewal

Ilion, My Childhood, My Memories

Otsego Street, Pre-Urban Renewal

East Main Street – Looking West, Pre-Urban Renewal

Ilion, My Childhood, My Memories

115

First Street off Otsego Street looking West towards the Oddfellows Temple.
Pre-Urban Renewal

Aerial view of Ilion High School – note the wing to the right where I spent
my Junior High school days.

The old A&P on Central Avenue

Franks Super Market near the corner of Hakes Rd and Main Street

Ilion, My Childhood, My Memories

Can't you hear the music playing and feel the excitement of running to this truck, waiting in line with the other kids, money in hand, until it was your turn to buy some delicious ice cream treat.

Otsego Street looking North Pre-Urban Renewal

Main Street looking West Pre-Urban Renewal

The old North End steel bridge over the canal out of Ilion

IT'S CLOSING — The Ilion P & C will close its doors on Saturday after almost 30 years of business in the area at the location. A Syracuse official for the company said the because of the expansion of the Herkimer store. No layoffs are planned as a result of the move. (Telegram Photo)

Many a high school teenager worked at these Ilion stores

Loblaws new location Post-Urban Renewal

Throwback Thursday takes you back to 1930 inside of Powers News on Main Street in Ilion (Courtesy of Ilion Free Public Library)

National Auto Store on Main Street Pre-Urban Renewal

Main Street Pre-Urban Renewal

Main Street looking East at Union Street

Ilion, My Childhood, My Memories

Wilcox Hotaling Block Pre-Urban Renewal, note the Utica Daily Press office below

Ilion, My Childhood, My Memories

Russell Park Playground and Pavilion

Union Street view from Main Street Pre-Urban Renewal

Powers News Pre-Urban Renewal looking North from Union Street

Throwback Thursday – Old Ilion School bus – called the Omnibus – dated 1880. Note the ski runners and horses pulling it. (Courtesy of Ilion Free Public Library)

48 Years In Business
Klippel's Variety Store -

Ilion's only Variety store on West Hll, Klippel's, will close its doors after 48 successful years in business. Built in 1929 by Fred Klippel, the store opened originally to sell groceries, school supplies, baby items, penny candy, auto accessories consisting of oil, tires, and had the only gasoline pumps on the hill. It's soda fountain was popular then, especially with teenagers and it remained the only original operating fountain in Ilion. The auto accessories were discontinued after about ten year.

Mr. Klippel originally operated his store with the help of his Mother, Mrs. Mary Klippel and his sister Allie. After Fred's mothers death, he was joined by his wife, Clara and daughter Beatrice and her husband, Leon Billings. They continued to operate their store supplying their friendly customer service to three generations of Ilionites. It also became a favorite morning break for many of the local delivery men of fresh baked goods, pies, cakes and bread, donuts; so popular in those days.

Klippel's has always been a favorite spot for children. It was always a convenient place for the students at West Hill School to spend their allowance or get rid of excess pennies. It supplied those important an dmost popular items such as bubble gum, baseball cards and penny candy, and also the patience so necessary (when waiting for children to make up their minds).

After the death of Fred Klippel, in 1965, Mrs. Clara Klippel and daughter Beatrice and her husband Leon continued operating the store. Mr. Billings death occured in 1975. Having kept their store active since, then, Mrs. Klippel and Beatrice will now retire from their busy schedule.

Richard K. Powers, Realtor transacted the sale to Robert and Shirley Torbitt who will operate "Torbitts Quality Meats and Groceries." Thomas A. Morris is acting Attorney for the Sale. An SBA Loan was obtained thru the Oneida National Bank, Ilion Branch.

The Sentinel, February 1952 – Local Advertisements

Ilion During Urban Renewal

The following pictures are highlighting the demolition needed during Ilion's Urban renewal. The source for the material can be found at this website:

https://nyheritage.org/collections/ilion-urban-renewal-collection

The start of Demolition, note the Christmas decoration overhead

View From Union Street Looking North

View from the West Side of Otsego Street

Ilion, My Childhood, My Memories

129

View From Central Avenue Looking South

View From East State Street looking South East

View From W. Main Street Looking Southwest – how many of you remember going into the shoe store and having your feet measured on the old metal Brannock foot measuring device.

View From W. Main Street Looking Southwest

View From Otsego Street Looking Northwest

View From Otsego Street Looking Southwest

View From Otsego Street Looking Southwest

The Odd Fellows Temple was among
the first buildings to come down.

View of the Odd Fellows Temple Looking Northwest on the Corner of Morgan and First, think of the history being torn down

View From Main Street Looking West

View of Main Street Looking Southwest

View From Main Street Looking Southwest

View From Main Street Looking East

Chomp! Chomp! Chomp!

View from Otsego Street Looking North Toward Main Street

Historical Facts about Ilion

- The village of Ilion is situated on the south bank of the Mohawk River in the town of German Flats. Settled in 1725 by Palatinate Germans, it was known successively as German Flats, Morgan's Landing, and Remington's Corners before incorporation as Ilion (for ancient Ilion, or Ilium [Troy]) in 1852.
- There was an early settlement called "New London" for which the western part of the present-day village was known for many years as "London."
- With the completion of the Erie Canal in 1825 the village began to flourish.
- In 1828 Eliphalet Remington (1793-1861) established a small factory for the manufacture of rifles.
- From 1830 to 1843 the village was known as Remington's Corners, and the first post office established in 1845 was named Remington.
- The village was incorporated under the name of Ilion in 1852 as Remington was opposed to the use of his name for the village.
- In 1856 the Remington company added the manufacture of farming tools, in 1870 sewing-machines and in 1874 typewriters.
- In 1874 with a population of about 2900 the village contained 2 hotels, a national bank, a brewery, a weekly newspaper and several schools and churches
- In 1910 with a population of about 6500, its principal manufactures were still the Remington typewriters and Remington firearms; other manufactures were filing cabinets and cases and library and office furniture (the Clark & Baker Co), knit goods, carriages and harness, and store fixtures. Many of these factories over the years harnessed the water of Steele's Creek to provide power for their machinery.
- By 1910 the village had a public library with about 13,500 volumes, a public hospital and a village hall and was served by the New York Central & Hudson River, West Shore railways, Utica & Mohawk Valley Electric railroad and the Erie Canal.
- The village owned its own water-works and its electric-lighting plant.
- By 1960 Ilion's population had grown to 10,199
- John F. Kennedy, 35th US President visits Ilion September 29, 1960
- In April 1965 a Master Plan was written to study a potential Urban Renewal Project for the Village of Ilion
- In 1966 Remington Arms celebrated 150 years in business.
- By 1974 the Urban Renewal project was complete and a ribbon cutting ceremony was held.
- By 2016 the downtown mall had converted into a medical facility with the addition of the Valley Family Health Center.

Ilion, My Childhood, My Memories

How Ilion got its name.

"Ilion" is a name for the ancient city of Troy. The area where Ilion is located was first settled by Palatine Germans under the Burnetsfield Patent around 1725. Settlers first took plots along Steele Creek, which flows into the Mohawk River. Gradually they built many mills along the creek. After the American Revolution, a small community was set up in the area named "New London". Ilion village still has buildings which use the name "London".

The community began to flourish starting around 1816 when Eliphalet Remington created his first rifle. He developed the Remington Arms manufacturing company. The community was stimulated in growth by the completion in 1825 of the Erie Canal, which completed area trade and connection with products from the Great Lakes region.

In 1843 a post office was desired, so the people had to choose a name. Remington refused to be the namesake of the village, and it was eventually named Ilion. A popular, yet unverified rumor is that the application said "Illium", but due to a misspelling or bad penmanship was interpreted as "Ilion".

The village of Ilion was incorporated in 1852. Ilion is one of only twelve villages in New York still incorporated under a charter, the others having incorporated or re-incorporated under the provisions of Village Law.
Source: https://en.wikipedia.org/wiki/Ilion,_New_York

According to Ilion's historian Mike Disotelle: David Devoe was the postmaster of the area before Ilion was incorporated. After a number of names were rejected including Vulcan, Fountain, and Remington (Eliphalet sternly refused to have the village named after him), Devoe recalled ancient Greek history and the city of Troy. Ilion was another name for Troy and upon Devoe's suggestion of Ilion, it was accepted as the official name of the newly incorporated village in 1852.

Ilion, My Childhood, My Memories

The 1882 Remington Fire Engine

By Allen W. Clark, 1st Assistant Fire Chief
Fellows Club Volunteer Fire Department and Ambulance Service in
Conneautville, Pennsylvania. Source:
http://herkimer.nygenweb.net/ilion/RemFireEng1.html

The Fellows Club Volunteer Fire Department and Ambulance Service in Conneautville, Pennsylvania owns a rare fire engine that fought many fires in the Borough of Conneautville for several years. The 1882 Remington Horse Operated Circular Pump Fire Engine was built by the famous Remington gun makers in 1882 at the Ilion, New York Remington Agricultural Works. There are now only two known fire engines left in the United States. The second one being kept on display in Phoenix, Arizona at the Hall of Flames Museum. [Editor's note: this second fire engine is also one based on the Howe Patent; however, it was built by the Rumsey Manufacturing Co. of St. Louis (see the Hall of Flame Fire Fighting Museum site for more info). Thus, the fire engine owned by the Fellows Club Volunteer Fire Department and Ambulance Service in Conneautville is the only Remington built fire engine that is known to exist today.

ORIGINAL ART, ADAPTED IN 1986 FROM AN 1890'S AD IN "HARPER'S MONTHLY MAGAZINE BY THE LATE FLINT, MICHIGAN ARTIST , MARK JENCA.

1890's Harper's Monthly Magazine
Ilion, My Childhood, My Memories

Late Flint, MI Artist, Mark Jenca's 1986 Adaptation

The Fellows Club Volunteer Fire Department and Ambulance Service in Conneautville, Pennsylvania owns a rare fire engine that fought many fires in the Borough of Conneautville for several years. The 1882 Remington Horse Operated Circular Pump Fire Engine was built by the famous Remington gun makers in 1882 at the Ilion, New York Remington Agricultural Works.

There are now only two known fire engines left in the United States. The second one being kept on display in Phoenix, Arizona at the Hall of Flames Museum. [Editor's note: this second fire engine is also one based on the Howe patent; however, it was built by the Rumsey Manufacturing Co. of St. Louis (see the Hall of Flame Fire Fighting Museum site for more info). Thus, the fire engine owned by the Fellows Club Volunteer Fire Department and Ambulance Service in Conneautville is the only Remington built fire engine that is known to exist today.

John F. Kennedy visits Ilion NY

John F Kennedy, the 35th president of the United States visits Ilion September 29, 1960, on a campaign stop prior to his election as President. Note the rain drops on his jacket as it was sprinkling that day. Source: Ilion Free Public Library

Ilion, My Childhood, My Memories

Appendix 1: Towpath – Old Remington Raceway

The Towpath has quite a history and was actually called the Remington Raceway (or the Raceway) that Remington Arms used as a water power source before electricity became predominant by the late 1800s. It was also used as a source of water for the Remington Arms Fire Department if accidents happened, which at that time they often did.

There were two raceways with one called the 'Upper' and the other the 'Lower'. The two ran parallel with Otsego Street all the way to the Remington Armory. By 1894, the raceway had become less important and since the completion of the village water works, the lower Raceway was no longer considered necessary and therefore was filled in. The filling in of the Raceway created several valuable building lots to be made available (source newspaper: Ilion Citizen 5-18-1894), resulting in several houses to be built on Otsego Street from Weber Ave to Benedict Ave during the late 1800s to early 1900s period.

Over the timeframe of 1900 to 1912 the Upper Raceway was being piped and filled in, and the grading of the Weber property was performed for the construction of the original Ilion High School (source: Ilion Citizen 9-5-1912).

The High School building was built in 1914, enlarged by two wings in 1925, and by the adding of the gymnasium in 1927. Gradually the Upper Raceway was filled in completely and remains today as what is known as the Towpath leading to the current day Ilion High School and as of 1940 becoming a popular thoroughfare for high school students (*source: Ilion Sentinel 12-19-1940).*

Remington Lower Raceway showing the Armory Hill Bandstand and what is today ('2021) the area along Otsego Street slightly north from where the Otsego Apartments are located (source: Ilion Free Public Library).

History is important. If you don't know history it is as if you were born yesterday. And if you were born yesterday, anyone up there in a position of power can tell you anything, and you have no way of checking up on it.
Howard Zinn

Appendix 2: The Ilion Pool

The following newspaper clippings are meant to serve as background information, and to chronicle some of the events that led to the creation of the new Ilion swimming pool, often referred to as the 'Big Pool'.

The Ilion Sentinel, 8/19/49 Editorial: DID WE CATCH IT!

Last week we spoke of the request of Frankfort swimming pool officials for lifeguards from Ilion to assist in handling crowds from Ilion at the Frankfort pool.

Reactions were immediate, varied and explosive.

The papers hadn't been out a half hour when Recreation Director Bart Shelley called to invite us to the pool which in his estimation is the cleanest it has ever been. Shelley felt we unjustly inferred the Ilion pool wasn't clean and added that his staff had worked extra hard to insure its cleanliness this year. (We have a hunch the boys may have been planning to drop us in the pool for first-hand experience.)

One of our prominent citizens stopped us on the street to inquire just what the matter was with us anyway. Always making noise about a pool," he went on. "When I was a kid, we used the Ilion Gorge for I swimming pool. What's the matter with the kids today? Can't they walk a half a mile or a mile anymore? Ilion doesn't need a new pool. The old one is all right."

At least one member of Ilion's official family protested our suggestion that mothers call members of the Village Board and ask them about a new pool.

"We're already called on everything from a cat in a tree to a tag on a car," he declared.

So at least people are talking pool. We still say, despite the respected opinion of one of our older citizens, that Ilion needs a new pool in a more centrally located spot. We believe that Shelley and his crew have worked long and hard with what they have to work with.

And after all, nothing in the way of a pool will be started until the Village starts in.

The Sentinel, 5/18/1950: … South Ilion Pool was original and deemed unsanitary prompting a new pool to be built. Estimated cost of new pool to be $54,000 with an annual cost to taxpayers of $1.20, to run for a ten-year period.

The Ilion Sentinel, 5/4/1950 bond for $65,000 will be voted on 6/10/50, mostly for the new Ilion Pool.

The Evening Telegram, 6/10/1950: ILION VOTES ON SWIMMING POOL Ilion—The Ilion Recreation Commission's year-long campaign for a new municipal swimming pool culminates today in a special election on a proposition to raise $65,000 for a pool in the Weber Pond area south of Ilion High School.

Sixty-two local taxpayers cast their votes at the Ilion Municipal Building between 9 a. m. today, when the polls were opened, and 10 o'clock. Voting will continue until 4 o'clock this afternoon.

The issue is whether or not the village board shall be empowered to issue $61,000 in municipal bonds payable over a period of not less than five years and transfer the additional $4,000 from surplus funds to finance construction o? a new pool on the Weber Pond site. If the proposition is approved by taxpayers, the village will commission an architect specializing in swimming pool construction to draw plans.

 The Sentinel, 3/8/1951: Village Board Will Consider All Bids at Special Session The new Village Board will Tuesday night to open sealed bids' on the Ilion swimming pool and whether the pool will be finished this summer will probably be answered that night.

The village has asked for sealed bids from contractors for the construction of the ovoid swimming pool, construction of a bathhouse, grading of the pool area and the Installation of other equipment.

Estimated cost of the project is $54,000.

The Evening Telegram, 9/4/1951: South Ilion Pool Closed Permanently
Ilion—The old South Ilion swimming pool is quiet today, not only because the youngsters have returned to school, but also because the recreation spot has been permanently closed as of yesterday.

No records were broken by this summer's attendance at the pool) as the long stretch of dry hot weather often accompanying the| season was not in evidence this| year. However, on the few hot days: average attendance was around 300, William Hall, lifeguard, estimated.

The Old South Ilion Swimming Pool

Next season swimmers will flock to the new pool which is being completed at the Weber Pond area. The pump house is finished and the pumps will be set this week. The bathhouse is complete except for some finishing inside and

Mayor Y. L. Power says that only the finishing of grounds and some painting remains to be done.

The Sentinel, 5/29/1952: THREE AWARDS ARE PLANNED FOR EACH RACE IN SWIM MEET

… Entries are now being taken by the Ilion Recreation Commission for the swimming and diving contest to be held in connection with the dedication of the new Ilion pool on June 23.

The Evening Telegram, 6/13/1952: Paint Brushes Fly, Landscape Work Sped at Ilion's New Pool

… The old pool in South Ilion has long been considered too small to handle the sports and also the location was not conducive to safe transportation of the many young people using the pool.

After much discussion of all plans submitted, planners of the Village Board decided to submit it to the voters. Plans for the outdoor pool were approved, a bond issue was also decided upon. Cost of the pool to date is approximately $77,500.

The egg-shaped pool was planned and designed by Wesley Blintz, swimming pool architect of Lansing, Mich., and is two and one-half times larger than the South Ilion pool. Water from Steele Creek, or from the village water system, will be used to fill the pool which holds a quarter of a million gallons of water and will require about six and one-half hours to fill.

The deepest end will be nine feet deep and the shallow end three feet. The pool is 105 feet long, 70 feet at the widest point in comparison with the 80 by 34 feet dimensions of the South Ilion Pool.

Appendix 3: The Auction of Remington Arms

The following text was provided by Mike Disotelle, the Historian of the Ilion Free Public Library.

During the mid to late 1870s until 1886, Remington had a cash flow problem. The company literally printed their own scrip and by 1882 officials were selling bonds to generate cash as shown in this image.

In April of 1886, E. Remington & Sons, as the company was called at the time, went into receivership, but for all intents and purposes the business went bankrupt. Two Ilion businessmen, Addison Brill and A.N. Russell, were court appointed receivers to stabilize Remington until it was sold at auction in 1888.

E. Remington & Sons fell victim to unscrupulous big business moguls of the late 1800s that have become known as "Robber Barons." (*Robber Baron, a pejorative term for one of the powerful 19th-century American industrialists and financiers who made fortunes by monopolizing huge industries through the formation of trusts, usually engaging in unethical business practices, exploiting workers, and paying little heed to their customers or competition.*)

Winchester and Hartley colluded with each other to make sure they "stole" Remington with their unethical business methods. One does wonder if antitrust legislation had already been made law, which was just a couple years away (1890), then perhaps this acquisition would have been disallowed. An Ilion Citizen newspaper article questioned the purchase of Remington with the headline "Is it a Gun Trust."

Remington was originally auctioned for $152,000, but the judge ruled that auction invalid and ordered another auction, most likely due to that absurd amount even for the late 1800s. The second auction was almost as bad, with a paltry $200,000 as the final accepted purchase price.

If you think about it, Remington was a nice complement for Marcellus Hartley who already owned an ammunition plant and was in cahoots with Winchester. What a way to corner the gun/ammunition market!

Hartley took advantage of Remington's cash flow problem, who by the way, had to sell bonds, to help pay off debt. These bonds are in the Ilion Library Historical Room's collection.

This is a Copy of the Remington Bond that is held in the Ilion Free Public Library historical collection.

It is difficult to assess Remington finances at the time, because company '**scrip**' was printed to pay employees (*Company scrip is a substitute for government-issued legal tender or currency issued by a company to pay its employees*).

The Remington Family was known for their impeccable reputation and local merchants accepted the company scrip. Therefore, when Addison Brill and A.N. Russell were appointed receivers of Remington during the financial crisis of 1886, the financial audit was very demanding because of the company's accounting practices.

Copy of Remington & Sons company Scrip written to employees. Local merchants knowing Remington's impeccable reputation would accept this as money in exchange for goods.

200 YEARS OF REMINGTON'S HISTORY

Remington 200 Year History Advertisement, 200 years of its history can be found at this website: https://www.zippia.com/remington-arms-careers-774993/history/

Remington Arms Company, Ilion NY

Appendix 4: Firsts for Ilion, NY

The following can be found here: http://herkimer.nygenweb.net/ilion.html
The CENTENNIAL BOOK - "ILION 1852 - 1952" – **Firsts for Ilion**

"Ilion seems to be a healthy place for the development of genius..." Editorial comment. Ilion Citizen 12-31-1875

1. The Remington Armory is first in age, or oldest, of present-day gun factories - 1816.
2. E. Remington and Sons was the first to use steel in the fabrication of gun barrels - Early 1820's.
3. E. Remington and Sons was first to manufacture by machinery and to export gun locks in America - 1846.
4. E. Remington and Sons was the first to manufacture and export military firearms. It and its successor, Remington Arms Inc., is also the first in the number of governments supplied; has manufactured the greatest number of patterns of firearms in the world; and has received the greatest number of firearms awards for excellence - 1846 to date.
5. E. Remington and Sons was first to drill gun barrels from a solid bar (Harpers Ferry musket); "then followed the drilling of small-bore barrels from solid steel, the drilling of double-barrel shot-guns from one piece of steel, the drilling of fluid steel and nickel steel barrel all done for the first time in this country at the Ilion shops. Harper's Ferry muskets - 1850.
6. E. Remington and Sons was first to manufacture self-cocking revolver - 1850's.
7. E. Remington and Sons was first to manufacture double action revolvers - 1856.
8. E. Remington and Sons, in 1857, claimed to be first in quality of barrels manufactured - 1857.
9. Remington Armory was first in number of gun barrels for muzzle and breech-loaders manufactured.
10. The first model of a Yale lock, opened with a flat key, was made in Ilion - about 1851.
11. The first machine for cutting, drying and packing matches by one operation was made in the Ilion plant - about 1854.
12. The first woman to have a desk job appointment in a federal government department was from Ilion, Miss Jane Douglass - 1862.
13. The first 100 velocipedes made in the United States were made at the Remington plant - about 1868.
14. The first successful propulsion of canal boats by steam was accomplished by E. Remington and Sons - 1870's.
15. Hoes, rakes and forks were first made by the rolling system at the Remington Agricultural Works - 1870.
16. E. Remington and Sons were the first to manufacture a commercially successful typewriter - 1873.

17. The model of James P. Lee's rifle, the first military rifle with bolt action, was made in Ilion. (Central Box Magazine) - 1870's.
18. The Rabbeth spindle for cotton machinery was invented and first made in the Remington plant - about 1878.
19. E. Remington and Sons introduced the first typewriter, model 2, writing both capital and small letters - 1878.
20. E. Remington and Sons was first to light by electricity, Schenectady, home of General Electric. Parker Systems were also installed in Utica, Dolgeville, Cohoes, Oswego, Rome and other places - 1880's.
21. The first test for high power ammunition for firearms was made at Ilion - 1880's (?).
22. The hay tedder was developed at the Remington Agriculture Works - About 1880.
23. The first Woman's Relief Corps in the State of New York was organized in Ilion - 1883.
24. The Ilion Citizen was the first newspaper in the world to be printed by electric power - 1884.
25. The Ilion Citizen was the first newspaper to be set mechanically - 1884.
26. The first Savage gun was made in Ilion - 1885.
27. The first Mauser gun was designed in Ilion - 1885.
28. The drop cabinet for typewriters was invented in the Ilion plant - 1886.
29. The Ilion Citizen was the first newspaper to be justified mechanically - 1893.
30. The Remington Standard Typewriter developed and introduced the first automatic ribbon reverse - 1896.
31. The Remington Standard Typewriter developed and introduced the first decimal tabulator - 1898.
32. The first 220 yard Straightway Race run indoors was run in the Typewriter plant - 1906.
33. The first move and donations toward the Baseball Hall of Fame was started in Ilion - 1917.
34. The first Treasury T award in New York State and the second in the nation for 10% or more pay roll deduction (for purchase of government savings bonds) by 90% of the people employed was awarded to Ilion - 1943.

Other machines perfected and manufactured here include special sewing machines; the Naylor battery gun; a portable gun for throwing a life line into upper floors of a burning building, also between ship and shore; agricultural implements of original type or made in original ways; the Remington steam street car. For a more complete list, reference may be made to the "Remington Centennial Book 1816-1916."

Other "Firsts" which have been developed elsewhere but have been or are being manufactured in Ilion include:
35. The first visible typewriter, the Yetman Transmitting Typewriter, was brought to Ilion and manufactured for several years - 1890's - 1906.

Ilion, My Childhood, My Memories

Accounting Machine Firsts manufactured by Remington Rand include:
36. First Vertical Adding and Subtracting Typewriter Accounting machine - 1908.
37. First Visible Descriptive Vertical Adding and Subtracting machine - 1910.
38. First Cross Computing descriptive machine - 1914.
39. First Automatic Electric Carriage return on bookkeeping machine - 1924.
40. First Front Feed carriage - 1926.
41. First completely Electrified Descriptive Accounting machine - 1932.
42. First completely Electrified Automatic Balance Accounting machine - 1939.

Tabulating machine firsts include:
43. First Punch ever to combine automatic feed and touch method of operation - 1916.
44. First Tabulator ever to accumulate and print sub and grand totals - 1923.
45. First combined punch and typewriter - as the bookkeeping machine types, a card is automatically punched - 1925.
46. First Tabulator ever to print words as well as amounts - 1925.
47. First machine ever to translate punched holes into words as well as amounts and print them across the face of the card - 1930.
48. First Instantaneous Summary Card Punch - 1931.
49. First Automatic Verifying Machine - 1932.
50. First Alphabetical Tabulator with Instantaneous Summary Punch - 1933.
51. First Printing Multiplying Punch - 1935.
52. First Multi-Control Reproducing Punch - 1938.
53. First Posting Interpreter - 1942.
54. First Multi-Stage Selector - 1942.
55. First Interfiling Reproducing Punch - 1943.
56. First Collating Reproducer - 1947.
57. First Card-o-Matic Punch - 1952.

Index

Flat top Guide Comb   15
Friends

- Hailston, Alan   72, 73, 75, 76, 110
- Helmer, Mike   34, 35, 38, 70
- Jeffries, Jim   38, 50
- Layaw, Joel   57, 59
- Outtrim, Dale   49

Golden Bomber   88

Herkimer County Community College   91
Hiraeth   102

Ilion Alma Mater   73
Ilion Armory Cemetery   ii, 82
Ilion Fire Station   94, 96, 97, 112
Ilion Old Baldy   82-84, 86-88
Ilion Russell Park   82, 124
Ilion Russell Park Bowl   82
Ilion Schools

- High School   18, 19, 22, 72, 73, 76, 82-84, 87, 88, 101, 116, 142, 145
- North Street School   159,160
- Weber Ave Elementary School   87, 142
- West Hill Elementary School   25, 32-34, 36, 39, 57, 64, 160

Ilion Streets

- Benedict Ave   8, 12, 15, 18-20, 22, 23, 25, 26, 142
- Central Ave   1, 94, 112, 113, 117, 130
- First Street   93, 97, 116
- Hoefler Ave   91
- Main Street (East, West)   3, 18, 57, 58, 93, 95, 110, 112-115, 117, 119, 121, 122, 124, 131, 134-136
- Marshall Ave   91
- North Fourth Ave   25, 26, 30, 34, 36, 39, 44, 50, 56, 62, 79, 158
- Otsego Street   8, 9, 12, 18-20, 22, 95, 107, 110, 113, 115, 116, 118, 129, 132, 133, 136, 142, 143
- Rand Street   57
- Weisbecker Hill   31, 75
- West River Street   1, 5, 8
- Union Street   93, 122, 124, 125, 129

Johnny Seven One Man Army Gun   17
Johnson's Paste Wax   66, 67

Kennedy, John F.   137, 141

North Fourth Ave, Ilion – Google Earth Street View

My 2nd grade class Picture at North Street School.

That's me standing to the left of the teacher, hands in pocket and ears flopping in the wind! Source: Author's photo collection.

Ilion, My Childhood, My Memories

About the Author:

Kevin Hall is a husband, father, and grandfather. Hall is 65 years old, born March 1957 in Herkimer NY. Besides his parents, Hall had three brothers and two sisters. Hall lives with his wife in Rush NY, a suburb of Rochester, where he has 2 married children and 6 grand-children. Hall is currently retired, after enjoying a 40-year career with: Remington Arms (4 yrs.), Eastman Kodak (17 yrs.) and the Xerox Corporation (19 yrs.).

A native of Ilion, Hall attended 3 different elementary schools – North Street, Remington Plant and then graduating West Hill. Hall attended Ilion Junior High through the end of eighth grade and moved with his family to Minnesota, where Hall attended and graduated from Rosemount Senior High School in 1975.

Hall lived in Ilion from 1957 to 1971, then again from 1976 – 1981. From 1971 – 1975 Hall lived in Rosemount Minnesota, and in Richmond Illinois for part of '76, where he married his wife. Hall attended Herkimer County Community College - Computer Science program and Brockport State College – Business and economics program.

A nation that forgets its past has no future. – Winston Churchill

Ilion, My Childhood, My Memories

Made in the USA
Columbia, SC
12 December 2024

49055129R10093